MIND YOU, I'VE SAID NOTHING !

Mind you, I've said nothing!

FORAYS IN THE IRISH REPUBLIC

by

HONOR TRACY

Robert B Luce, Inc.
Washington, D.C.

Published in the United States of America in 1968

Library of Congress Catalog Card Number 68-20390
Printed in Great Britain

To
NORAH
and
ROBIN, CATRIONA, ELIZABETH
Her Children

CONTENTS

I

FOREBODINGS

IS writing about Ireland so risky an enterprise? Does it really require, if not the courage of a lion, at least the hide of a rhinoceros? I had recently announced that I was starting on an Irish sketch-book, and my friends had keened and lamented as if my corpse already lay on the bier. Tough assignment, they remarked, shaking their heads. Explosive subject! they went on. Sooner you than me! they croaked. You'll catch it! they added, and now their faces brightened a little.

They were all Irish.

Until they all piped up in their chorus of woe I had not supposed that the path ahead was fraught with such peril. Any one, it seemed to me, who earns his living outside of the Twenty-Six Counties may write freely of Ireland without fear of the consequences. There may, of course, be a few anonymous threats of murder: or a letter, nicely phrased and warmly expressed, describing the pleasure thousands would feel in watching the author writhe in flames at the stake: an odd fulmination from the pulpit is possible and even likely: or a scurrilous outburst in one of the more pious and less readable newspapers. Sometimes a book will be publicly burned or some writer perhaps made the object of a vilifying campaign by the Department of External Affairs; but treatment of this kind is reserved for those of outstanding merit. There are bound to be declarations that the writer will never be allowed in the country again; and there may also be a little snowstorm of writs for libel, for the Irish are a sensitive race and never more so than when a prospect of damages, enticing as the fabled crock of gold, looms in the background.

I should have thought, however, that any normally robust person would take such trifles, apart from the writs, in his stride. It would be a grave pity, a singular collapse, were he to do anything else, for these attacks, these howls of rage are only partly real, or rather, like so much that is Irish, are real and unreal at one and the same time. Over and over again the stranger in Ireland will be bewildered to see two gentlemen, who have been savaging each other in print, in company, wreathed in smiles and with their arms figuratively about each other's neck: and the writer who has been bid never to set foot on Irish soil again will receive a kindly welcome as soon as he does.

The difficulty, indeed the impossibility, of writing about Ireland in such a way as to win the approval of Irishmen, may arise from the ambiguity of their own feelings towards her. If she is criticized, they are publicly furious and privately amused: if praised, they are outwardly pleased while inwardly condemning the writer as a fool. One could argue all night as to which of their attitudes is the " real " one: probably neither: the one sure thing is that what vexes them most is when Ireland is not mentioned at all.

On the other hand the writs must be taken seriously, for there is no ambiguity whatever in the Irish feeling about easy money, or the hope of it. The earthiness of the true Irishman—as distinct from the Anglo-Irish settler—is something not usually recognized abroad and which, if trouble is to be avoided, should ever be borne in mind. Peoples are often inclined to offer a picture of themselves to the world that is in direct contradiction to the reality and which again, out of ignorance or laziness, the world will sometimes accept. The picture is not always more attractive than the reality: the point is that it is not true to life, being

dreamily compounded from those elements in which the
people sense themselves to be lacking. Indeed it is merely
the extension on a wide, collective scale of a common human
weakness. Who does not know those irreproachable maiden
ladies who are somehow convinced that they are very
naughty and very daring? or those engaging idlers who
expect at any moment to be carried off in their prime from
overwork? Thus the English love to think themselves as
cool and calm and prosaic, whereas they are nervous and
highly strung and romantic often to the point of inconvenience. The Italians stress their martial valour and
aptness for the fray whereas among their many splendid
qualities these are the least in evidence. And in the same way
the Irish have patiently over the centuries built up a legend
of their spirituality and disinterestedness and disdain of
worldly things that does not march with the facts or, for
that matter, impinge on them at any point.

The writer who knows his Ireland, then, even while he
appreciates the brilliance of their imagery and the sustained
force of their invective, will make merry over the pile of
abusive and threatening screeds on his desk, from which a
colleague less experienced and reared in a suaver tradition
would recoil in dismay: but those little solicitors' letters he
will handle gingerly, as if they had been a red-hot coal.

The motives which lead Irishmen to insist on the perils
awaiting the writer on Ireland are somewhat harder to
disentangle. He cannot surely believe in them. Better than
any one he must be aware how little there is behind all the
fuss and fizz and the rant and roar. Most likely he hopes to
scare the raider away, in the manner of those tribes who
shout and scream and brandish their weapons at the sight
of the enemy, only to retire with good grace on finding it
all in vain. For any one who writes of Ireland is a probable
enemy and especially he who brings to the subject an alien

point of view. It is remarkable how the Irishman shrinks from being seen in different lights and considered by standards different from his own. His reason may tell him that Ireland has no more to be ashamed of than any other country: and that outside opinions of her may be no juster than those internally accepted: but it is no good, he winces at the very idea of the inspection.

It may be that a wretched history has the same effect on a race as a wretched childhood on an individual, whom we often find unable to endure criticism from others while carrying on a merciless criticism of himself. Any one who has ventured to find a fault in Ireland and is then taken up by one of her infuriated sons will notice that the interview tends to divide itself in three phases. First he hears, as he would expect, that he is ill-informed, ignorant, illiterate, if not actually malicious and a liar. If he is an Englishman he will be reminded of the salient crimes in English history in such a way as to make him feel personally responsible for each. When all passion has been volatilized by the soothing action of words, and not before, the native kindness reappears and the pair settle down to a friendly discussion.

" Mind you, there was nothing personal in all that," the Irishman will remark.

At this point as often as not he suggests they both go round the corner for a drink. As soon as the first drink has disappeared something reminds him that a bird never flew on one wing and he orders another: will indeed order a succession of drinks on the basis of similar aphorisms, all perfectly true in themselves: and lastly in no time at all he will lace into Ireland himself and lash the poor thing with a tongue like the flail of God, while the erstwhile critic sits there beside him and feebly protests.

Sometimes this order of things is reversed. The Irishman now is one of the liberal, rational kind and he sidles up to our critic with a worldly, sophisticated, we-see-through-it-all-don't-we air about him that is misleading and dangerous. He has amazingly broad views on politics and an enlightened detachment from all religious dogma: he dismisses his fellow countrymen as a bunch of crooks and comedians: and in general he talks so well, so placidly and so tolerantly, that the innocent stranger may fall into the error of replying in similar vein. Cases are known where a mistake of this kind has ended in bloodshed.

Another bogey employed by Irishmen to scare writers away is the prospect of complete and awful and humiliating failure. One thing he may be sure of is that he knows nothing about Ireland and can never hope to understand her. This boggy little piece of land with its few inhabitants, lying forlorn in the ocean, washed by rain and curtained by mist, in grave danger of being overlooked by the outer world were it not for its frequent and lively toots on the horn, has special—indeed unique—qualities which defy penetration. The writer may be a man of wide experience, with a know-ledge of many people and many lands, but it will be of no use to him here. The secret will elude him for ever: he can only make a fool of himself by attempting to probe it. His time will be better spent, his readers get better value for their money, if he directs his attention to countries that are simple and crude and obvious, like England.

This argument would be more daunting if it were not so familiar, if it were not a favourite consolation of every small and isolated and insignificant community that was ever known. It is what in our young days Nanny would call " trying to make yourself interesting " and would visit severely, as she used to visit all free and joyous play of the imagination. We should not follow her example and tear down with ruthless hands the little flag that flutters there so bravely at the masthead; but nor should we allow ourselves to be silenced before we have opened our mouths. Let the writer on Ireland accept her specialness and apartness and the limitations of his own understanding with humility, and let him none the less pluck up courage and struggle to portray the land and its people in a way intelligible at least to the world outside and to such Irishmen as have been perverted by contact with it.

There remains a final shot in the Irishman's locker. He has dealt at some length with the dangers and difficulties of writing this book: he now asserts that no one will buy the book when it is written. Who on earth wants to read about Ireland? and what in heaven's name is there to be said about her? As far as the second point is concerned, there will be days and days on end when the writer fully agrees with it. He will scratch his head and wonder if, when he signed the contract, he was possibly out of his mind. George Moore somewhere quotes a legend to the effect that Ireland has the power of making herself small as a pig's back to her enemies, while to her friends she displays every enchantment and delight. If it were true, it would simplify matters considerably. It would settle the question, so persistent, so vexing to our minds, of whether we loved Ireland or hated her. Am I in Paradise? or riding the back of a pig? we should ask ourselves and the answer would define our attitude once and for all. Unhappily the legend would seem to be false. It is one of Ireland's little tricks to be a land of sweetness and magic at one moment and the back of a pig at the next; and in the phase of the pig there is nothing to be done but to curl up and ride bravely along until things improve.

But it is scarcely true to say that nobody wants to read about Ireland. In Ireland itself, for example, it may be questioned if any one really wants to read about anything else. The people are wrapped up in themselves to an almost morbid degree: everything sooner or later must be related to them. Correspondences will begin in the newspapers about some problem in the world outside—say the developments in the Far East—and continue on a note of sweetness and reason and indifference until somebody finds a parallel of one kind or another in Irish affairs, no matter how far-fetched it may be, and there is an animated free-for-all at once. Ireland! Ireland! Ireland! the word falls on the ear with the gentle persistence of rain on the shores of Kerry. Any book on the burning subject then, even by an ignorant alien, is sure of eager perusers who will read it from cove to cover in an ecstasy of contradiction and pass an enjoyable hour or so in listing the errors of fact, faults of grammar, misprints, foolish opinions and other evidences of incapacity on the part of writer, printer and publisher.

More surprising is the amount of interest taken by Ireland's neighbour over the water. This interest is often rooted in misconception, for no one has so completely and loyally accepted Ireland's idea of herself as some of the English have. Their notions verge almost upon the extravagant: they see the Irish as witty, poetic, reckless, mystical, passionately devoted to forlorn hopes and impossible causes, the possessors of a wonderful sense of humour and, of course, charming: there'll always be an Ireland, if England has anything to say in the matter. It is delightful to see people who are better placed historically and geographically than any others to know the truth so cheerfully content with the legend. And yet our Irishman is still far from pleased. A shadow falls across his face and he sets up an angry mutter in which we perhaps may catch the words " stage Irishmen " and " colourful natives." In his eyes, to have swallowed so much of Ireland's own make-believe is merely another and a signal example of English effrontery.

Now that brings me to something else: " stage Irishry." The writer on Ireland is certain to be accused of indulging in it. He need only note down an amusing remark or describe an engaging character to be indignantly told he has embroidered, if not invented, the whole affair. Once I asked a Dublin policeman to tell me the exact time, having a reason for wanting the exact time and no other, and he replied at once without the ghost of a smile that the exact time was between two and three. I was enchanted by this, reflecting that a city where time was of that timeless order was the only good place to live nowadays. So pleased was I with that answer, so grateful to the man who made it, that I gave the story in a broadcast; and sure enough by the next post came an angry letter from an Irish listener with a scathing reference to " that apocryphal cop who never existed except on the boards of the Abbey Theatre."

On another occasion I printed a story which I overheard one Irishman telling to another. It was a nice little story and one that breathed out the very soul of Ireland. In the days of petrol-rationing some men were asking the landlord of a pub where they could get petrol on the black market. A Sergeant of police heard them at it and advised them to go up the road to a certain garage; and they thanked him profusely and set off. In no time at all they were back, crestfallen, to report a failure. Hardly able to believe his ears, the Sergeant asked if they had revealed who sent them; and they answered that they had.

" There's Ireland for you ! " said the policeman, bitterly. " No respect for the law at all."

Both the man who told the story and the man who listened to it were chuckling together with the greatest delight. And I myself on one occasion, being in dire need of black-market petrol, had consulted the local police as the source and fountain of it and had not been disappointed. The story not only illustrated in a charming way the humanity of Irish officials but gave an accurate picture of Irish methods of distribution. No sooner was it down in black and white, however, than the usual furious letter arrived accusing me of lies and distortion and inquiring sardonically why I hadn't thrown in a " Begorrah ! " while I was about it. I hadn't done so because I knew better. The Irish may sometimes say Bejabbers and Bejasus and Begob but they do not say Begorrah and, for some reason, they are very insistent on this point. But what was there in the story to make this correspondent boil over ? And why was he so sure that I had made it up ? That is a thing which no one in Ireland need ever do when it comes to racy dialogue or piquant episode; the most fertile imagination could not hope to compete with real life. It is only when the writer yields to the entreaties of Irish patriots and attempts to write of Ireland " as she really is "—that is, as of an orderly modern state, making giant strides forward in science, art, education and social welfare—that he may have to fall back on the inventive faculty.

Not only do " stage " Irishmen abound to this day but they are far pleasanter than the other kind. There is a remote little railway station somewhere in the west, visited once or twice in the day by small erratic trains. The station-master is a genial and cultivated man, very strong in conversation and a great one to welcome you back. The delight that transfigures his face as you step from the train, whether real or assumed, plays an important part in your coming. On the technical side of affairs, however, he is a little less sure of himself. To find out how to get from his station to another with a change or so in between involves a protracted conference, an anxious scrutiny of time-tables, many of them obsolete, and in some cases a prepaid telegram to the nearest junction. On these occasions, for that matter, he has been known to break down and suggest that it were better to go by car. Once I returned from a council of this sort, cheered and amused and happy as usual but not without misgivings about the journey we had mapped out together. There was to be waiting here and waiting there, and while it may be better to travel hopefully than to arrive, it is hard to do so when the chances of any arrival at all seem roughly to be ten to one. The mind of the station-master, too, was not completely at rest, for late that evening there was a scrabbling at the front door and a little barefoot child handed in an envelope marked Personal and Urgent. Inside was a note from him which said: " Try to find out is the 12.30 from ——— still running, it would save you that long wait at ——— ."

I had no crystal ball and was therefore unable to pursue the inquiry. The journey was carried out on the following day, step by horrible step exactly as we had planned it. The station-master is a " stage " Irishman of the purest water, of course, and I love him dearly. His virtue, his peculiarly Irish virtue, is to take an interest, a preponderant one even, in the human aspect of his work. He cares about you and he wants you to travel agreeably. After you leave him he does not dismiss your predicament from his mind but continues to brood over it, searching his heart as to whether the advice he has given is the best available. He comes to the conclusion that a certain possibility has been overlooked. Owing to flaws in technical equipment he is not himself able to say if it is more than a possibility; but he takes the trouble to sit down and write a note to send his little messenger over stony paths in the darkness with it.

I find in this man a positive good in not only his human but his functional capacity. I delight in the artistry which transforms the act of making a journey into something we never dreamed it could be. To me he appears an ornament to the country and not a disgrace. Others will exclaim at once, if all station-masters were like him where should we be? but that is simply hysteria. My correspondent, if he is

willing to concede the fellow any existence at all outside my
own disordered brain, would be deeply ashamed of him.
He would no doubt prefer him to snap out the hours of
trains with a teutonic precision, as one of these days he may.

The writer's duty, however, is to observe and not to
anticipate.

The problems that lay ahead, I thought, were not the
ones put forward by my nerve-ridden Irish friends. It was
not the thought of obloquy or assassination or even litigation
that kept me tossing and turning but rather a fear that I
should miss the core of the thing itself. For while the faults
and follies and absurdities of Ireland are plain to see and
amusing to describe, she has a mysterious sweetness of her
own that is hard to define and still more so to communicate.
There is a magic about the country in some of her moods
which runs through the fingers like water as one tries to lay
hold of it. Then, too, there is the question of perspective.
She dreams along in a world of her own, in a little bubble
of her own imagining, frail no doubt as bubbles are but
attractive. How to describe her in relation to the rest of
mankind and as a part of it, and not still appear to be treating
her vulgarly as a joke? There is a nice problem of mental
adjustment involved, and one that is possibly not to be
teased out. It does not take the outsider long to notice that
the agony of the world is curtained off in a highly successful
way. Major calamities are duly reported in the newspapers
but they are not much discussed, and what discussion does
take place is often so fresh and fanciful, so completely
divorced—as it appears to the newcomer—from any reality
as to lift them once and for all from the plane of material
happening. At first one may throw oneself joyously into the
prevailing mental climate, eager for a vacation not only
from dire events but as it were from consciousness itself; but
over a period it induces a malaise bordering on despair.

I once met a lady in Dublin who felt quite sure that no one so far had got the atomic bomb. There had only been one of these engines, she explained; it was invented by the Germans and discovered by some G.I.'s as they picked their way through the ruins of Berlin. The Americans had carried it off and dropped it on Hiroshima but had not yet managed to make one for themselves. The processes of mind, the stages of reasoning, by which this conclusion was reached she was not prepared to disclose; but there was no doubt that the clamour about atomic warfare was leaving her serenely unmoved. It was not so much the lady's interpretation of events which seemed to me typical of Ireland, however, for she was clearly in a class by herself. It was the spirited resistance she put up to any argument which might appear to invalidate it. Of the second bomb on Nagasaki, of Bikini, of the tests carried out in various countries before and since, it was useless to speak as she waved them blandly aside. Listening to her as she calmly and reasonably developed her thesis, I had, as so often in Ireland, the sense of talking to some one for whom facts were not in any way real.

This question of fact was another of the spectres hovering in my path. In every book there should be a fact here and there or the writer is charged with aimless frivolity. But facts in Ireland are very peculiar things. They are rarely allowed to spoil the sweep and flow of conversation: the crabbing effect they have on good talk is eliminated almost entirely. I do not believe myself that the Irishman conveniently ignores their existence, as sometimes is said, so much as that he is blithely unaware of it. He soars above their uninviting surfaces on the wing of his fancy. Who then would answer my questions truthfully, who would supply me with that modicum of sober and accurate information required to give my book a serious air? No one, as far as I knew.

And if facts are elusive and shadowy things in Ireland,

opinions are more so. An Irishman, sober, will say not what
he thinks but what he believes you would like him to think;
he is a man of honeyed words, anxious to flatter and soothe,
cajole and caress. When he has taken a jar or two and is in
the mood for trailing his coat, he will say whatever he judges
will give the greatest offence. In neither case does he reveal
his own true thoughts if, to be sure, he has any. He would
be in dread lest you quoted him and the story went round
and he got the name of a bold outspoken fellow, which might
be bad for business. And then again so many Irishmen find
an innocent glee in misleading and deceiving for its own sake.
Obfuscation is the rule, and while it may seem a little foolish
at times, there is no doubt that it makes for a great deal of
fun. It cultivates too a sharpness of ear, a feeling for half-tones
and shades and subtleties, and a wary alertness that would
be worth its weight in gold should one ever be lost in a jungle.

Writing about Ireland, like living in Ireland, is a challenge
to the integrity. It is not a robust, noisy challenge but a
quiet, insidious, deadly one; the howls and catcalls, the
verbal brickbats and the figurative rotten eggs are neither
here nor there. It is as if you had to walk steadily over a
quaking bog with will-o-the-wisps nodding and beckoning
from every point of the compass, luring you gaily on towards
pools where you might lie buried for ever. Now and again
in the course of this hazardous expedition the thought must
come: but what am I doing this *for*? why am I not warmly
tucked up in my bed? and you find no reasonable answer.
Reason in any case is not your strong suit; you would not
be carrying on with Ireland at all if it were. In fact you can
find no answer at all but must just plod sturdily on: sustained
and fortified, if there is a drop of Irish blood in your veins,
by the thought of the general disappointment and fury if you
manage to get across.

II

BACK TO DUBLIN

THESE ideas flitted across my mind as I sat in the
saloon of the packet bound for Dun Laoghaire,
creating a mood of despondency and alarm. I did
not think I should be able to perform the wire-walking turn
that lay ahead. There were reasons for this beyond the
difficulties involved in the turn itself. The time was between
three and four in the morning, when the blood flows slowly
and the future appears as a likely succession of defeats and
disasters. The night was stormy and the little packet tossed
and panted, wheezed and groaned, as if she were nearing
the end of her endurance; and while the fury of wind and
waves left me unmoved, the sufferings of other passengers
did not. In the chair next to mine sat a pretty nun in blue
habit and starched white cap, an enamel bowl clasped in her
trembling hands, and murmured prayers, no doubt of an
oblatory nature, falling from her lips between one paroxysm
and the next. The poor white bonnet nodded and ducked,
waved wearily from side to side, while a sister nun in scarcely
better case looked on with compassion. The sight of this
girl who had shouldered the pain and the sin of the world
itself being floored by so risible and vulgar a complaint
turned one's thoughts to the vanity of human striving.

There was another reason yet for the diffidence of my
mood, a personal one and which would not be mentioned at
all except that on this short, uncomfortable voyage there was,
as it happened, to be granted me a peculiarly Irish consolation
and balm. Only two days before I had made a fool of myself,
publicly and on a generous scale. I had been invited to join

a broadcast Forum, one of those programmes where a panel of speakers, presumed intelligent, rap out authoritative or amusing answers to questions put by the audience: and in front of a crowded hall I had dried up, floundered, spluttered and covered myself with ignominy. It was one of those things which make little impression on the world at large, saddening friends for an hour or two, perhaps, and cheering enemies for slightly longer, but which burn like acid into the heart of the booby herself.

Now I sat in darkness of mind recalling the horrible evening stage by stage and reflecting bitterly on my incompetence. All at once the neat, spare figure of Cyril Cusack hove into sight with—there seemed a touch of the miracle in it—a bottle of Scotch protruding from his overcoat pocket. In no time at all, as the bottle passed from hand to hand, I was pouring the story into his kind and attentive ear; and when it was done I leant back, hungrily waiting for words of comfort however empty, banal and unfeeling these should be. But Cusack's face lit up.

"Didn't you do that audience a very good turn?" he cried. "Didn't they go home afterwards and say that clever London lady was a bigger fool than any of us? Won't they be grateful to you as long as they live?"

He went on to describe the downfalls and disgraces of his own career, the curtains rung down, the galleries that booed, the indignant stormings of box-offices, all very likely invented on the spur of the moment out of the warmth of his heart. Even if they were not, there was now no need of them; for what he had said was so probably true, he had shifted so finely the centre of gravity, that from that moment on I had never a twinge again. I clearly saw that audience, robbed of their evening pleasure to some extent, yet returning home with a new and firmer assurance of their own powers, thanks to me and my little collapse. His Irish eye perceiving at once the heart of the matter, his Irish tongue finding just the words to fall on the blister like drops of oil, Mr. Cusack restored to me there and then my peace of mind; and, better still, reminded me of the beautiful Irish response to distress in a fellow creature.

I took fresh heart: some of the doubts and misgivings melted away: and it struck me there was after all a chance of finding happiness in Ireland, could one only arrange to be completely and disastrously and permanently in trouble.

Presently the voyage came to an end. The toy harbour of Dun Laoghaire looked as quiet and sleepy as ever when the ship pulled in through the dark blue of the winter dawn. The sailing craft that tossed idly up and down on the ripples with a row of seagulls perched round each gunwale seemed more at home in it than the packet which was creating almost a vulgar disturbance. Down on the jetty with leisurely movements, no one anxious to kill himself, men were preparing to bring up the gangways. Eager to get away, the passengers had collected on deck and jammed themselves into a mass in which it was impossible to move or breathe. There were priests and nuns, shaggy-haired boys, women bowed under the weight of children and brown paper parcels, members of the ascendancy, purple of cheek and flowing of whisker, all wedged together in a cross and hungry mob. The sea which had buffeted the little ship so rudely on the way over now subsided into an oily calm: lights were coming out one by one like stars over Killiney hill: a smudge of pink along the horizon showed that the morning was not far away. From a church ashore came the sound of a bell chiming softly three times.

The people began pouring down the gangways. The customs examination that morning was both strict and lenient, in that everything down to the last paper bag had to be opened, yet nothing was searched. Gravely the

conductor showed the passengers into their carriages and
locked them in. A countryman home on holidays with all the
sophistication of England behind him launched into a tirade
against the land that locked its children in trains. Why was
it done ? No one knew. The conductor was appealed to
and readily explained that it was to keep them in and, at
the same time, to keep them out: which either mollified
the indignant countryman or stunned him, for he said no
more. Placidly the little green train set off for Dublin.

At Westland Row I put my luggage in the cloakroom and
went to an hotel for a good Irish breakfast. The bill of fare
offered orange juice and bacon and eggs. A forlorn waiter
in baggy trousers and dancing pumps brought a glass of sweet
fizzy orangeade, a piece of bacon like a sliver of brick and an
egg like a piece of dried sponge swimming together in a
lake of congealing fat, toast likewise of brick and a cracked
tea-pot from which gushed forth a brew the colour of ox
blood and tasting of seethed leather. I left them all there on
the table as silent witnesses to the truth that austerity is of
many kinds and returned to the cloakroom for the luggage,
only to find that it had closed up like a flower at sundown.
A notice chalked on the door said it would open again at
noon. A man standing by gave it as his opinion that it
would in fact open at half past three. His attention was
drawn to the notice.

" Don't mind it," he said.

The only man who could deal with the situation was the
Inspector, at that moment enjoying a cup of tea in the
buffet upstairs and who therefore should not be disturbed.
Another man standing by gave it as *his* opinion that a lady
should not be kept waiting for her luggage. We argued it
back and forth, striving to come to a just decision, and agreed
at last that the Inspector should be told at once but invited
to finish his cup. But he rose up immediately, leaving all,

and ran lightly downstairs waving a bunch of keys. The luggage was piled into a taxi with the help of every one in sight and the driver, disposing himself in a way that left him unable to see much of the road, began a lively account of how he'd nearly taxi'd a basket of Siamese cats to Sligo the week before and how, after long and delicate negotiation, the deal had fallen through on account of the expense.

It was a bright sunny day with small fleecy clouds scudding over the sky. Having left my things at the hotel I went for a walk. The first hours in Dublin are always delightful, for the city throws all it has at the newcomer, discreetly flattering, gently soothing, feeding at once the eye and the imagination. The airs of grace and of leisure have not departed even if the society which gave them birth is past and gone. It is a city of ghosts, but ghosts of the so newly dead that something of their earthly presence still lingers in the wide streets, the pleasant squares, that were their home; as you walk through them, you feel that Dublin still must be a bed of poetry and wit, almost you expect to see Yeats and A. E. passing each other in Merrion Square as in the famous cartoon, George Moore must at that moment be in Ely Place devoting one more scintillating page to the dissection of a friend or happily ruminating how best to enrage a neighbour. But the truth is you are looking at a lovely shell; the old glory has departed, a new one is not yet in sight. The Georgian houses of rosy brick on the good side of the river are full of Government people, commercial firms and business-like doctors; and many of those on the other have turned into slums.

Sometimes, however, it is wise to be content with the appearance of things, especially in Dublin where surfaces as a rule are agreeable. The more superficial your approach is here, the happier you will be. Pleasant ways of speech and manner have not yet been forgotten; the gentleness, the warmth, the quick sympathy with the stranger, turn every chance contact into a source of pleasure. Wrapped about by kindness like a grub in a cocoon, entranced by the city's lovely face, the returned traveller falls into a mood of uncritical enthusiasm. Fresh from the crazy world beyond, he feels that he has entered a little haven of peace and joy. In spite of the teaching of experience he will, if he is not careful, start prattling about Holy Ireland and the Irish way of life.

I am myself immune from this particular error because years ago I asked an old lady in whose judgement I had confidence if in fact Ireland could be said to be holy: and she replied at once, with a burst of seagull laughter, Holy Ireland me bottom ! The phrase was perhaps not an elegant one, should not perhaps be reproduced here, but it expressed briefly and forcibly something that in a groping way I had long been trying to formulate: and made so deep an impression on my mind that to this day I cannot hear the words *Holy Ireland* without those two others bobbing up and arranging themselves, although of course they are left unspoken, as a complement. From the gaiety, the intoxication even, the sense of wrinkles being gently eased away of that first impact, I am not yet immune nor wish to be.

Once more the beauty of Dublin revealed itself intense and theatrical in the magic light of Ireland that is softer and gentler and yet strangely more luminous than the light of other places. At the corner of Suffolk Street crouched the same old flower lady with the same old battered hat and ancient shawl, the rings in her ears and the engaging grin. The Liffey sparkled gold as it hurried along on its way to the sea and the ramshackle houses on either side, washed yellow and pink and blue, glowed in the sun like the streets of some Mediterranean port. Seagulls wheeled and swooped overhead with plaintive, childish cries and fat little barges puffed downstream laden with barrels of stout for England. A ragged woman with wild red curls falling about her shoulders and her feet thrust into carpet slippers made a bee-line for me from the other side of the road. I thought she was coming to beg for I seem to act as a magnet for beggars and always give them what I can spare with a vague idea of encouraging them; but she was only going to tell me, on a sudden impulse, how hard it was to work in the house without any hot water.

" Difficult, indeed," I said, and she was pleased to find that her position was understood and undertook to remember me in her prayers.

Nothing was changed: how pleasant! Even the auction rooms apparently were offering the same wares as in the summer before: the dusty bric-a-brac, the pots and pans, the harp with the broken strings, the immense straw hat with red and yellow cherries dripping from the brim, had still not found a purchaser. Bowed over the second-hand books were the early bookworms, who lifted their heads now and again to stare out into the sunlit street with little pale blinking eyes. In other windows were row upon row of plaster saints with meaningless faces, painted in nursery shades of pink and blue: the Infant of Prague with top-heavy crown, St. Elizabeth and her roses, the Redeemer Himself pulling aside His garments to show the Sacred Heart, cushiony and crimson as a ripe strawberry. A woman stood arguing with the vendor of a statuette of Blessed Martin de Porres.

" He's not very black."

" That's the blackest we do at three and six. There's a darker one for seven shillings."

" Dear enough ! "

" Then take the three and sixpenny one. Sure, Blessed Martin wasn't really black at all."

" Oh he was black all right," said the woman, annoyed.
' He was black. But give me the three and sixpenny, so."

Round the corner in O'Connell Street still another note
was struck. Here were the cinemas, with the bills announcing
films that glorified everything Ireland pretends to despise,
where later on there would be long, patient, avid queues.
Here were ice-cream parlours with American-sounding names
and cheap smart shops. Lord Nelson stood at the top of his
pillar, gazing imperiously over the capital of the Republic;
he ought of course to come down but it would make work and
cost money and people have grown attached to him. And
there were the hoardings with the posters to remind you of
the hard little core of rancour behind all the smiles and
geniality. Alien Publications Threaten our Irish Christian
Heritage ! End Partition: Come on Sunday and Hear
Speakers from Occupied Ireland ! Away with Compulsory
English ! I am a West Briton: I Take my Opinions from the
British Press ! and others too, which being written in Irish
withhold their secret for ever from most of the passers-by.

At one end stood the imposing pile of the Gresham
Hotel, haunt of businessmen from England and the more
prosperous of the Irish clergy. Half-way down was the
General Post Office where once a quite remarkable number
of heroes barricaded themselves in and where now severe
young men, wearing the badge of temperance, push stamps
across the counter and gaze with no friendly eye on the
ragged figures who seem to regard it as a second home.
And up and down the street went the jostling, bustling,
plebeian crowd, girls with their hair worn in imitation of
the reigning Hollywood star, grubby little boys screaming
the names of newspapers, pale spotty youths trudging along
with a Legion of Mary barrow . . .

I turned aside and, having bought the morning newspapers, made my way into a snug that had long been a

favourite because of the unlikelihood of meeting a familiar face in it. In the greenish twilight, with an air of having never moved since the beginning of time, sat still the three old gentlemen with the bottle noses and the split boots, and the seedy bowler hats which they would gravely remove at the entrance of a woman. At no matter what time of day, except in the Holy Hour, they were to be found in session. No word ever passed between them; it was impossible to judge if they were acquainted or not. Silent and absorbed they sat, each with a pint of stout at his elbow; nor did they break their silence when the stout was gone but merely brought their glasses down on the table with a sharp tap and the barman appeared at once with a rag to wipe the table in one hand and a fresh pint of stout in the other.

They were three of the finest and purest drinkers in Dublin: oblivious of their surroundings, of the venerable leather seats with horsehair bursting profusely from every crack, of the rickety wooden table with the collecting box set there by the Holy Ghost Fathers for the Chinese Mission, of the perpetual dusk in the room: disdainful of conversation, indifferent to the passing of time, they sat and swallowed with never the faintest flicker of pleasure discernible in their features.

The sense of a continuity in things to which their presence gave rise was heightened by the first glance at the newspaper. The race horse switched or doped, the new list of banned books, the flattering message from an American Senator of Irish descent, the denunciation by a bishop of pillion-riding as liable to reveal the leg: it was all there, almost word for word as in the last Dublin newspaper I had read months ago. But there was one grievous gap, alas! for even in Ireland changes creep in and time is remorseless, and the voice of Father Devane, S.J., was hushed and stilled for ever.

That reverend gentleman had lived in a state of constant

dread lest the Irish mind be contaminated by the materialist influx from the other side of the water; and while in the main he was very good about it, holding his peace for months on end, at intervals it would be too much for him, would all come boiling up in his mind, he must snatch up his pen or explode and a bewildering flow of arguments, figures and invective would result. For some reason—or rather, by the purest chance—my arrivals in Dublin regularly coincided with an outburst either from Father Devane or from Father Felim O Briain, who is happily still with us and of whom, therefore, more shall be said in due place; so that I would be somewhat in the position of a cinema-goer who, having just been shown to his seat, rises almost immediately to exclaim " but this is where I came in ! " Neither spoke to-day: Father Devane was where for one reason or another the importing of English Sunday newspapers into Ireland would hardly vex him further: Father Felim, no doubt, was fruitfully meditating in Galway City.

This little touch of the strange and the unwonted was further underlined by the absence, to-day, of a Fuss. There is usually a Fuss of some kind going on in Ireland. There has to be to make life interesting. As a rule the Fuss is launched by politicians in the first place, with the willing support of local government bodies throughout the country, and tenderly kept alive by the press. For example, by arrangement between the British and Dutch Governments a number of Dutch airmen may be posted for training to Northern Ireland. The politicians, casting about for something to do, will decide that this is a flagrant violation of Irish rights and Irish soil—it is apparently their belief that if they behave for long enough as if the Border were not there it will lose heart and vanish of its own accord—and thus tantamount to an act of armed aggression. Diplomatic protests will be made, county councils will cable sharply to similar bodies in Holland, causing perhaps a few honest Dutch brows to wrinkle in amazement, and a boycott of Dutch goods will be announced. The public goes on its way completely unmoved and a little later a Friendship with Holland week can be arranged, to show it was all in fun.

Again, the Fuss may be a feat of private engineering. A trouble-maker might write in to the papers under an assumed name to point out that a valuable picture in one of the public galleries was in need of restoration. This would be hotly denied by the authorities concerned and a merry little exchange would take place. There would be a resurgence of interest in art. The gallery, whose usual public consisted of a few coloured students from Trinity College, might suddenly be thronged: and the anxiety for one of Ireland's treasures increased by the discovery that the room containing it was suddenly closed for spring cleaning or reorganization or, perhaps, just closed, with the glass doors veiled in brown paper. That would be quite a good little Fuss, enjoyed by nearly all and harmful to none: for if many months later it were to happen that a discreet paragraph in the newspaper announced the return of the picture duly restored by the hand of a foreign expert, by that time another Fuss would be holding the public eye and the memory of earlier assertions and contradictions would be sponged from the public memory.

For the most entertaining Fuss, if not the biggest, of recent years the palm must go to none other than Father Felim himself. It began with his letting fly out of the blue on the subject of liberalism and socialism which, he contended, not only led to economic absolutism and totalitarianism respectively but also to loose living, abortion, free love, homosexuality and divorce. Among the black sheep of these two "isms," which he apparently linked together, he listed Voltaire, Rousseau, Bentham, Marx, Engels, Zola, Gide,

Russell and Proust. A hullabaloo broke out in the columns of the Protestant *Irish Times* and raged for weeks on end. The sturdy friar, impervious to all argument but his own, easily rode the storm, inducing in the mazed minds of some readers a condition bordering on vertigo; and the eyes of his chief opponents gradually took on a wavering, moonstruck look as of creatures lost among new and startling dimensions. In mercy at last the editor brought the thing to a close: and not long afterwards in Galway I was pleased to see Father Felim announcing a lecture to be called: *This Art Business— What is it?*

The papers to-day had nothing near so good. From one end to the other there was nothing to make one sit up and cry Ha! A social column revealed that an Irish lady novelist had arrived in Dublin and was staying at the Shelbourne: that a certain Doctor would be out of town for three weeks : that a Mrs. O'Reilly had removed from the South Circular Road to a house in Rathgar. A hairdresser announced his return from the South of France. A mouse had been found in a bottle of stout, causing nervous shock to the consumer. Damages were awarded. A country lad had batted his old da over the head with a loy with fatal results. An editorial explained to the world where it was going wrong. A bishop was appealing for funds. Or am I telescoping the events of years? I write from memory.

I went out into the sunlight again, the three old gentlemen gravely replacing their bowler hats as I did so. An hour remained before a luncheon appointment. I strolled back over the river and up Grafton Street, almost colliding at the top of it with an enemy, a small stout gentleman with the misleading appearance of a friendly teddy bear. I danced aside into a doorway to spare us both the embarrassment of cutting each other; but there was no need, for even at this early hour his eyes were set and staring, his features frozen

in a grimace of plethoric good will. The noon-tide Angelus
rang from the Carmelite Church and, vaguely making the
sign of the Cross, he reeled away out of sight into Mooney's
Bar.

A walk in Dublin is full of such encounters. They
perhaps explain the wary look in the eyes of Dubliners and
the strange crab-like sidle of the more nervous among them.
The streets bristle with danger. You may be mooching along,
intending no harm to a soul, at peace with heaven and earth.
Towards you comes a lank figure in hairy tweeds and battered
hat, one of Dublin's innumerable geniuses. From the air of
purpose in his bearing it is clear that he means to borrow a
pound. In many places the loan of a pound will purchase
immunity not only from further applications but from the
society of the borrower too and may thus be regarded as a
prudent investment; but in Dublin it has the strange power
of creating a bond between the parties that nothing seems
able to shake. Jesus, that old pound ! if I hadn't forgotten
every word about it ! would j'ever make it two, till next
Friday ? Once again Operation Snowball commences.

Here, then, a borrowing genius comes and just in time you
pull up, slap your forehead histrionically as if remembering
the milk on the stove, wheel about and make down a side-
turning as fast as your legs will carry you. A tall, distinguished
man coming out of a shop raises his hat and looks daggers.
Up to that moment you were not conscious of having offended
in any way, had cherished indeed the belief that you were
rather a favourite, but no sooner do you get that steely look
than you realize what is behind it. It flashes across your mind
that when you were last in Dublin you never went to see this
person. True, in order to do so you would first have taken
the train: and then the bus: and the trains and buses are
dovetailed brilliantly to miss each other: and then you would
have climbed up half a mountain, the last stretch over rock:

and it was pouring with rain every day. You have only to look at the curl of that long, thin nostril, the sit of that head on the shoulders, however, to see how inadequate the excuse would be.

" Good morning ! I'm back again," you quaver.

" Welcome. I had begun to think you were dead," and he passes on.

A new enemy, then, is added to those already recruited and quietly biding their time. Thoughtfully you proceed on your way, feeling ever so lightly bruised. The next familiar figure may be the writer of a satiric newspaper column. You are alive to this fellow and his little ways and in the ordinary course of events, in the full possession of your faculties, you would immediately take to your heels; but your brain has been clouded by the previous encounter and you suffer him to lead you away for a drink, kind and comforting as a boa constrictor with a baby. And how witty he is, how learned, how sympathetic and kindly disposed ! why do so many people declare that he is not a human being at all ? You leave him at last feeling greatly refreshed and encouraged. Nor does he forget you the minute your back is turned: he thinks about you, he ruminates in his lair, you have started a train of ideas and, in the course of the next day or so, he will devote a few blistering lines to your address.

For the present, however, you are under the impression that a new friend has been made to offset the new enemy; the balance of power, you fancy, remains what it was. Your defensive convolutions have brought you now in a circle to St. Stephens Green and you wander across to the little bridge for a moment of peace. You will stand and watch the willows trail their arms in the water and the merry ducks and the budding plants for a space before summoning up the resolve for another plunge. Some one has got there first and, with his elbows on the parapet, is staring gloomily down at the pond. Needless to say you know who it is but it does not matter, for this is one of the people in Dublin you love to see. At your cheery hail he swings round with a hunted look in his eyes: recognition, dismay, a flicker indeed of something fringing despair, pass swiftly over his face and at last there comes a forced, reluctant grin.

"Isn't it wonderful how you never take a step in Dublin without meeting some one you know?" he says.

It is perhaps the only village on earth that contains half a million souls: one great big unhappy family, as a Dublin writer cried out once, burying his face in his hands. And all the things I have mentioned duly happened this morning. Now I murmured something about having to hurry along and my friend smiled his relief as he urged me politely to stay. After only a few hours I was ceasing to be the homing traveller and becoming the uneasy resident. The transition from one state of mind to the other grows perceptibly smoother with every return: ultimately the mere sight of Dublin hills on the horizon will call forth a whimper of apprehension.

I went on my way, keeping a sharp, swivelling eye to the weather.

III

PARTY POLITICS

THE following days were filled with the rigours of hunting for a place in which to live. The advertisement columns were daily combed for something which should be pleasant and clean and yet not reserved for a quiet Protestant gentleman. Agents were visited, where the opportunity of savouring once again the Irish gift cf lyrical description was enjoyed. Wildgoose chases, set afoot by the kindness of friends, occupied much of the time.

Years ago when I first lived in Dublin I had a piece of great good luck in this matter of housing and it has left me a little hard to please. When it happened I had been staying for several weeks in some Luxury Service Flats and was approaching despair. The nature of the luxury concerned, the basis for the allegation of service, were secrets that will remain for ever inviolate. It was a square, ugly building that had been run hastily up in one of Dublin's charming old streets, ruled by a manager with the appearance and the behaviour of a plain-clothes policeman; and the flats were dank, dirty rooms with windows that would not open and doors that would not shut, where once in a while a troglodyte languidly passed a mop over the linoleum on the floor.

The place I escaped into was hardly more than a mousehole and consisted of two tiny rooms, a bed-sitting-workroom and a bath-dining-room-kitchen. A board came down over the bath and provided a table during the day and when the time came for a bath it was hoisted up and secured with a cord: a match was tremulously applied to the gas and the ancient geyser, groaning and creaking, would collect its powers and send forth a thread of scalding water, while the meter was bribed with penny after penny. Beside the bath was a gas-stove, through one of whose rings there filtered an intermittent trickle of gas and on which I cooked my simple meals. This was in the period of rationing when the gas was turned off for so many hours a day and only a faint breath of it was left in the taps, and the glimmer-man roamed the city trying to divine in which house a clandestine kettle might be a-boil, and making sudden, excited little pounces. I was spared these temptations and hazards, for even at the peak hour, when gas whistled through other pipes like a tropical wind, I never coaxed more than a sigh from mine; and the question, posed afresh every time, of whether the heat would be equal to the tasks before it, added a further interest to cooking.

What gave this apartment its unique fascination was in the first place its owner, and next, the fluid arrangements she made about its furniture. She was a rosy, twinkling, candid old lady with original views which, contrary to Irish practice, she saw no reason to hide, and very considerable powers of expression. She occupied the rooms below mine and below those again were her business premises where she carried on a flourishing trade in antiques and *objets d'art*. An artist to her finger-tips, she was never wholly content with the result of anything she undertook and thus regarded the furnishing of my little den as only provisional. A core of permanence, it is true, there was. The bed was unmolested throughout the whole of my tenancy: so was the great mirror with the beautiful frame of gilt leaves that hung over the fireplace, reflecting the events in the street outside and imparting to them the romantic interest of things seen at a remove: and so was the wicker armchair in the kitchen which leaned gently to one side like a willow tree in the wind and which, with any shifting of weight, would slowly and deliberately topple over, depositing the incumbent on the floor.

But for the rest there was a constant coming and going. Chairs, tables, even cupboards would be whisked away and replaced by others: the pictures on the walls, all of them good, were changed almost weekly. Often I would come in to find my little home smiling at me with a completely altered face; and late one night, returning merry and confused from a revel, I thought I had stumbled into the wrong building altogether, so radical were the changes effected in my absence. Sometimes this busy lady, with so much on her mind, would make a mistake and by an oversight instal in my room an article which was really destined for the repair shop. I would go to pick up a jug and find only the handle of it in my grasp, or I would sit on a three-legged chair and all would crash to the ground together while a peal of eldritch laughter from the floor below would intimate that the joke was being enjoyed.

The shop downstairs was another source of pleasure. There was not an inch of space in the whole room and it was in the care of a female genius who could lay her hand on anything at a moment's notice. This wonderful woman would plunge into a heap of shawls, fans, pokers and tongs, and majolica and emerge with just that tumbler, with the photograph of King Edward VII cunningly superimposed, for which you had long been pining. With the help of a cheerful small girl she used to fall upon the place and clean and dust and rearrange the multitudes of wares in groups more enticing yet; and often, as she had just completed this, would come a shout of greeting from the door and the chubby little proprietress entered, followed by men reeling under the weight of wooden boxes and crates, she having been to an auction. A frenzied consultation would follow; and somehow the capacity of the room would be stretched still further to admit of the incoming stock. One of the many sidelines of my landlady's venture was the marketing in summer time of fresh produce from her country estate, so that one suddenly came on a clutch of brown eggs or a punnet of raspberries or a twist of spring onions nestling among the folds of a velvet cape or tucked away in a box of Georgian spoons; and for a moment a little country breeze seemed to blow through the fusty air.

In return for a tiny rent I was not only housed but befriended and entertained. There was even a translation service, free of charge, for any scraps of Irish that might creep into an official letter, for the cheerful small girl had only just left school and still was able to make it out. The only snag in the arrangement was that, pent up at the top of a flight of steep, narrow stairs I could neither see who approached my door nor hope to avoid them; and the essence of reasonable living in Dublin is to be able to do both of these things. And at night when all was quiet I lay in bed listening to the crumbling and collapsing of the old walls and meditating on the transitory nature of things; and sure enough two years later the house came down, having first, however, been sold to a business man.

A suitable flat was discovered at last with a view of the Wicklow mountains from the bathroom window. It had high, airy rooms, elegant furniture and lilac trees in the garden as well as a double means of egress. The landlord was a stout, florid person with very strong views on the lower classes. He was also rather keen in business, for the rent of the place was given on the agent's book in pounds and he at once translated it into guineas, remarking that errors would creep in; and when the agent himself telephoned that evening I knew at once from the cautious note in his voice that something was up.

"I didn't know at all," he said, after a preliminary

skirting flourish, " that you were such an old friend of the landlord."

Nor did I.

" He feels that in the circumstances the arrangement is strictly a personal one, and we ought not to insist on our fee."

My previous acquaintance with the landlord had begun and ended with seeing him lunch one day at a neighbouring table in Jammet's; and this I unkindly revealed.

" Is that right ? " said the agent, delightedly. " I thought that was about it. He's a terror, that fellow. He has every agent in Dublin mystified."

The landlord was defeated on this occasion by my sending a cheque directly to the agent who abstracted his fee and remitted the balance; and he was very indignant, saying that if he had only known there were to be complications he would have given the flat to another prospective client, who was practically on her knees for it.

I began my tenancy with certain reservations of feeling towards this landlord, therefore, but time was to show how wrong I had been to judge him in haste. It turned out that he was intensely devout: that he had each of his houses blessed by the priest before a tenant came in: and that once every year he made the pilgrimage to Lough Derg which, by the severity of its fasting and the length of its vigils, is said to be the most arduous in Europe. The thought of that poor fat man stumbling barefoot over the sharp stones was almost too much, but he assured me once that on no account would he miss it: the only concession he made to his comfort was to go on a Tuesday, thus keeping clear of the riff-raff that went at the week-end.

A home being found, the next thing was to give the expected party. To give a party in Dublin is no trifling matter. It is, in fact, an exercise from which all but the stoutest hearts might recoil. To begin with, it is impossible to keep it dark; every one will know it is being given and if he has not been asked he will wish to know why. The solution that might occur here to a superficial mind would be to hire the Shelbourne rooms and ask everybody. This, however, would not answer at all. There are a whole lot of people in Dublin who positively decline, under any circumstances whatever, to meet no end of others. They will wait angrily for the invitation, rehearsing what they mean to say should it fail to arrive; but when it does, far from being mollified, they immediately set to work finding out who else has been asked and take umbrage at that. Mr. X is staggered that it should be supposed he would ever be seen, even dead, with Mr. Y: Mr. Y always thought you would have had more taste and discretion than to ask him with Mr. X. The mere fact of your having perhaps spent a year or so in foreign parts and thus having lost a little the thread of Dublin life will be no excuse.

Lapses of memory are not the only or even the worst dangers that lie ahead and steps may, after all, be taken to avoid them. Projecting yourself into times gone by with the single-minded tenacity of Proust himself, you may recall in its every detail the feud between Y and X from the first little tiff to the point where legal proceedings were started: you strike their names from your list, which already begins to look like a game of noughts and crosses, and substitute those of Z and W. What now you have failed to take into account is the dynamic nature of Dublin society. During your absence Z and Y may easily have become the closest of bosom friends and spend each alternate week-end bicycling together round the Bog of Allen. On the other hand W and Z are now at daggers drawn and, within twenty-four hours of the invitation being issued, are telling every one they meet what they think of you, their wives adding that naturally you did it on purpose.

At the thought of the wives my hand began ever so slightly to tremble. It was almost enough to make me abandon the venture forthwith. There is a peculiar, if not mysterious, quality about the Dublin wife which makes her, however estimable as a woman, a total irrelevance as a spouse. One simply cannot understand the principle on which she was selected; not only does she fail to appear as a complement, or even as a foil, to her husband but she has the knack of transforming him into a stranger before one's very eyes; and it is over these social gatherings that she casts her longest shadow.

How Dublin wives manage to exert their repressive influence on a festive occasion is another mystery, for they usually segregate themselves at one end of the room while the men form into closed rings at the other. Two separate shows appear to be going on at the same time, as in a mammoth circus. On the one side are the women, sipping and chattering together like a flock of starlings and all dolled up in feathers, veils, flowers, fancy gloves and immensely high-heeled shoes. On the other are the men, in tweedy jackets and unpressed trousers, telling each other stories in low furtive tones. The ring-master may run from one to the other as much as he likes but he will never succeed in bringing about a fusion. Nevertheless the women contrive by secret means of their own and without so much as glancing in their direction to frustrate their husbands' natural desire to get drunk as fast as they can. The mere fact of their presence spells certain social failure. Their conversation restricts itself as a rule to babies, clothes and bridge; and they are still more critical, still more on the defensive, still more anxious to feel slighted or snubbed than their male counterparts.

Then how would it be to give a party for bachelors only ? The audacity of the notion quite took away the breath. Imagination boggled and shied at the thought of what the ladies would say. And for this very reason the plan suggested itself as a shrewd stroke of policy; for where people devote so much ingenuity, talent and wit to creating scandal out of the air, they are often sadly adrift when there is something solid to work on.

In this connexion instinct was supported by memory. I remembered how once at a Dublin party, an affair of evening coffee and buns, the hostess had suddenly rustled from the room signalling the ladies to follow by grimaces and eyebrow-liftings as if it had been a dinner. I had not met this Dublin custom before (nor, if it comes to that, have I since) and, mistrusting my eyes, remained where I was. No later than luncheon time on the following day reports came rolling in of the embroidered accounts of this simple event, and the ingenious constructions placed upon it, that were winging their way round Dublin with a kingfisher's speed. It seemed to me now that by inviting a number of single men I should merely live up to the reputation of nymphomaniac so firmly and easily founded that evening of years ago: and the pleasure would be further spiced by the thought of the wives as they raked their exhausted vocabularies for words that should do it justice.

But I had hardly begun to savour the delightful idea when I saw an objection. It had nothing to do with public opinion but arose out of the weakness of the flesh and a certain haziness as to the terms of my lease. I was not sure how my landlord would stand with the insurance people, were his chairs to be laid in sticks and his piano silenced with cataracts of stout; and I was approaching a time of life when an hour or two of sleep every night is desirable. There is a wild poetry in the continuing orgy, the mad drive through the night to another house or to some illicit snug in the country, the unforeseen breakfast on the other side of the Wicklow hills or even in Mullingar; but as years go by the honeyed

prose of pillow and blanket pushes its claim with steadily
waxing urgency.

I put the bachelors' party firmly out of my mind. Now
I spoke sharply to myself, pointing out that this was not a
chore or a battle or a baptism of fire but a happy reunion of
dear old friends. I must not become hysterical. For nearly
an hour I had sat pencil and paper in hand and there was
nothing to show for it yet. Down went two names in slow,
careful writing and were rapidly crossed out again. They
wouldn't do. Then I wrote another, with a question mark
after it: the trouble in this case, once again, was the wife.
She was much addicted to the society of notables and unless
I had " got " Somerset Maugham or an equivalent she would
wonder why she was asked.

Memory flickered uneasily again: hadn't something
awkward once happened to me in her house ? Heavens, yes:
there was the time that she netted a well-known artist with
whom I had been acquainted in London. I had arrived to
find him standing all alone in the middle of the room, his
moustaches nervously twitching, and we fell into a rather
protracted conversation. Presently our hostess came up and
remarked in piercing tones: " Now then ! You needn't
think you are going to monopolize the lion of the evening ! "

It was the first intimation I had received that this was
a lion-hunt and not a party at all. Every head in the room
turned towards us at that clarion cry: the artist blushed as I
have seldom seen a lion—and never an artist—blush: I
stood convicted and labelled. And such was my shame and
despair that to a social *faux pas* I added the sin of deceit, for
as the dentists and lawyers and auctioneers who were
circling the lion in faintly resentful bewilderment came up
and begged me to reveal at last who and what he was, I
told them all that I had simply no idea: had never heard of
him in my life before.

Shuddering at the recollection, I crossed the pair of them out. In a sudden feverish burst I wrote down six other names. They belonged to people who never quarelled with any one, never found fault or indulged in malicious gossip: kind sweet safe Christian people, all made of pure gold. Until I saw them listed there in black and white one after the other I had not realized Dublin contained half so many: I reflected upon it: one thought gave way to another, a drowsiness stole over me and, yawning, I crossed them all out again.

The task was proving too much for my powers and I laid it aside. Instead I began to make an estimate of the provisions and drinks that would be required. Twenty people should be asked, if I had to pull their names out of a hat: but here again I fetched up against the vagaries of local etiquette. It is no uncommon thing, for example, for those invited to conceal their intentions until the party begins. Perhaps they have never found out what the letters R.S.V.P. stand for; it is a custom of the pious in Ireland to insert a D.V. after the announcement of a forthcoming marriage or other social event, and they may assume that R.S.V.P. too merely implies submission to the Divine Will. Perhaps, again, they are holding their hands in case something better turns up; or perhaps they want to burst in on the company as a delightful surprise. The social secretary of a foreign Embassy in Dublin once told me that one of his duties, when the Ambassador entertained, was to telephone round on the day itself and ask the distinguished *invités* if they meant to come; so that there is no need for the private citizen to feel hurt by what appears to be neglect or to put it down to his own insignificance. And if in spite of this he should feel hurt, his self-esteem will be smoothed down again by the numbers who come without being asked at all.

And for what time, pray, should they be asked? and could it be said to matter? The announcement " cocktails

6-8 " on a card has to Irish eyes a meaning quite other than that usually accepted in the western world; or rather, it has no meaning at all. It does not make it safe for you to arrange anything else for nine o'clock or ten or to assume that you will be in bed before the break of day.

Whom to ask: how to persuade them to come: how to prevail on them to go: what to get in: how to live the whole thing down afterwards . . . . I had been absently doodling, repeating over and over again the little square box which is the only thing I can draw, when suddenly I chanced to look up into the mirror over the fire-place. A stranger with seamed face and dishevelled hair stared out of it with the haggard look of one who has watched all night by a sick man's bed. In the rush of pity, surprise and concern the scales dropped from my eyes and the solution revealed itself in all its fine simplicity. It was there of course all the time, but had been overlooked, and is given now in the hope that it may be useful to others similarly placed. The idea was, briefly, not to give a party at all, either then or later. There was to be no entertaining of Dubliners in the mass at any time or on any pretext whatsoever.

I was staggered to think it had never occurred to me before.

IV

SOME PEOPLE

CRIMONY is not the only note in the Irish scale
although it is sounded so often as to make it appear
at least the dominant one. It goes hand in hand
with a gay nonchalance which time and again saves the day.
In between the clouds of spleen and gloom are little patches
of fun both madder and merrier than to be found elsewhere.
The Irish too, like Madame de Staël, are great ones for
rescuing those they have previously drowned.

Human beings after all have a right to be happy in their
own way and the Irish enjoy their spleen as much as and
possibly more than their mirth. Perhaps this is why many of
them feel so sadly adrift when they go to London. From a
distance England appears like El Dorado, spiritually as well
as materially. Once I stood on Dun Laoghaire pier with a
scientist, watching the little silver aeroplane shooting out
across the sea to London; and he cried aloud with an
exceedingly bitter voice, " To think that sanity is only an
hour and a half away ! " Yet he had worked in London,
had given up his prospects there to return to Dublin and still
was free to leave again if he chose; and there were numbers
of others in similar case. I cannot help feeling that it was
just the sanity of which my friend had spoken that grated on
their nerves. No one properly boils with rage in England: in
that well-ordered country there are few pretexts for savage,
delightful indignation, and worst of all, when the occasion for
such does arise people usually do something sensible about it.
The Irishman thus is left with an awful hunger gnawing at his
vitals, which only a return to the land of his birth can satisfy.

48

Yes, there are many cheerful and amiable Irish qualities.
If I were looking for some one to personify them the choice
would undoubtedly fall on the novelist, Peadar O'Donnell.
Not every one would agree. Peadar has often been discussed
in my hearing with severity. It has been said that he is a
Bolshevik, and also that he is a playboy. He has also been
described as a pietist and as having more business acumen
than a cartload of levantines joined together. Such criticisms
on the whole are more revealing of the critics themselves
than of Peadar; and in any case once you are with him you
forget everything but the pleasure of his company.

He is short and smiling and of a friendly truculence. A
ousled mop of white hair surmounts a face that he himself
has likened to that of an old sheep. Two piercing blue eyes
look out at the human race with immense affection and
approval from under beetling brows; and from his lips in a
good northern accent come a stream of the most preposterous
stories that ever were heard. These stories he tells with a quiet
assurance, a masterly development of theme and an attention
to detail which carry his listeners away. Only much later
when you attempt to pass them on to others, people begin
to look gravely and you suddenly come to your senses.

There are two stories in the collection which are particularly splendid. One concerns an attempt on Peadar's
life during the troubled times. The would-be assassin was a
venerable priest, who apparently shot from his hip with one
hand while holding his breviary in the other, pacing up and
down in front of the church meanwhile and tranquilly
reading his office. The other was of an I.R.A. man who was
tried for murder and successfully pleaded insanity. Peadar
and his friends, who had supervised and indeed suggested the
defence, then rescued the hero from his asylum by a series of
carefully planned and ingenious moves, only to find to their
horrified dismay that he was in fact a raging lunatic. I

could never hope to relate these anecdotes in their full beauty, however, and it would be wicked to try.

Peadar surpassed himself once, when he drove me through themountains to Glendalough. Dublin, incidentally, possesses a great charm in that you so easily leave it behind and reach a wild lovely countryside. Even on the cliffs at Killiney or Howth with the blue waves tumbling drowsily about the rocks and the seagulls wheeling and swooping overhead, the dust of the city seems very far away. The inhabitants are quick to avail themselves of their chances and on a fine summer day row upon row of cars may be seen, windows and doors all carefully closed, the occupants staring fixedly at the view.

The road Peadar took wound up through bare tawny hills, past lonely farms and white-washed cottages, one splendid landscape following another until we came at last to the valley and drew up under the trees beside the water. The holy place was quiet and mysterious and gloomy. Dull green woods rose steeply above the shores of the lake, creating an atmosphere that was closed and oppressive. Every one behaved with immense decorum: no one hawked souvenirs or oranges or threw paper on the ground. A party of young men were solemnly taking their places in a boat to be rowed across to the cave where Kevin the hermit had once passed his time in meditation. A woman enamoured of the saintly man had followed him there, to his great impatience, and had presently been tumbled by him into the water and drowned: whether his subsequent canonization had been on account of this spirited deed or in spite of it, I cannot say. We dawdled on the bank until the sun began to go down and the uneasy brooding air of the place made itself still more felt, and then drove back to Dublin.

Throughout this little trip, which took up the whole of an afternoon, Peadar was never silent for more than a few moments' time. Considered simply as a feat of endurance, it was prodigious: what was still more remarkable, not the slightest falling-off in the quality of his conversation was ever to be noticed. At the end of it all he was as fresh and gay and lively as at the beginning: it was I who, my credulity taxed to the uttermost and my poor brain whirling, limped homewards a broken thing and immediately lay down to rest.

His political views defy analysis. Is he socialist or conservative, anarchist or liberal? Various of his utterances at different times lend colour to each of these conflicting possibilities. But he regularly goes to Mass and eats fish on Fridays and (so an enemy claims) says the rosary every night of his life. It does not matter very much: only fools and professionals are consistent in politics. By temperament he is a benevolent patriarch, the chieftain of a clan so big as to comprise the human race. A purely aristocratic sense of responsibility drives him on to fight for Irish potato-lifters in Scotland or for peasants in Spain or for the inhabitants of the Dublin slums.

At one period of my life this quality was the greatest blessing to me. There was no reason at all for him to take me on to the staff of the magazine that he was editing except that, for the moment, I was on the brink of starvation. He always inclined to the view that the needs of a person qualified him or her for employment; and it is said that once, asked to explain an apparently redundant pair of hands working for him, he replied, " It is a married man with four children."

Arriving one day in my little flat he found me sitting down to a simple, nourishing meal of boiled potatoes. Whether he had come with his mind made up, or took a swift decision at the sight of this dish, I do not know, but he offered me a job at the then magnificent rate of six pounds a week. Joyously I accepted and hurried out to buy some butter and take my boots to be mended.

The offices of this publication were in a house in O'Connell Street, down near the bridge, affording a pleasant

view over the Liffey. Beside the editor there was a staff of
three: an assistant editor (I was therefore to be known as the
editorial assistant), an accountant and the advertisement
manager. The last was a handsome young woman of placid
manners who brought whatever there was of calm and
method into the picturesque confusion of our lives. The
assistant editor heartily disliked any form of routine and
further had his reputation as the Don Juan of Dublin to
consider, so that much of his time was spent in following up
some romantic possibility or other: and once or twice it was
necessary to hide him in the inner sanctum while we fobbed
off an indignant lady with tales of his sudden departure for
London. He knew an astonishing amount of poetry by heart
and would declaim at great length with sweeping gestures
and a solemn intonation, particularly when we were trying
to draw his attention to some little oversight, such as the
failure to return corrected proofs to the printer.

"Ah, I'm nothing but a seagull spreading his wings in
flight," he would remark complacently, when at last we
broke through his defences.

The accountant was a truly outstanding personality, a
man of broad culture and humane disposition. His speech
was like the flight of a kingfisher, darting this way and that
and making heavy claims on the understanding of a less
agile-witted audience. He was also keenly observant. He
did not fail to notice that money was inclined to go out of the
office rather faster than it came in. This was not due to any
exaggerated liberality towards the contributors, who after all
had the honour of seeing themselves in print to reward them;
but rather to the fact that Peadar spread his wing over all
who were friendless or in need. Unemployed, men newly
released from gaol, lame ducks and mountebanks called to
see him and seldom if ever went empty away. Peadar
clearly regarded the moneys thus paid out as part of the

normal running expenses of a literary magazine, but on the whole the accountant dissociated himself from this view.

" God help us ! " was a favourite ejaculation of his.

He would stare haggardly at the books as if he thought they would bite.

Peadar's feudal generosity led to the only row we ever had. He has often called me a spy from the British Foreign Office, a reactionary, a dowager duchess and other names: but I am speaking of a row. I was going to London for a few days to try could I get some commissions, and on hearing this Peadar at once bestowed on me, in his princely way, a voucher for first-class return fare and five pounds to spend. Having thanked him warmly and humbly I set off in high feather, and of course blew every penny not only of Peadar's gift but of what I myself had collected for the journey. Shortly after my return, being greatly reduced, I sent in a bill for previous contributions to the review, only to learn that Peadar considered all accounts between us to have been settled by his act of munificence. Correspondence broke out and raged with a steady unfaltering violence possible only in Dublin: culminating in an aide-mémoire from me which opened with a prayer to the Devil to fly off with my employer, and went on to explain that had I understood the position I would not have travelled first-class: to which, not being a communist, I was unaccustomed. The battle was such a pleasure that I entirely forget who won: but when I met Peadar soon after the final burst, he was wreathed in smiles and our happy relations were never disturbed again.

The system on which we worked so closely followed that of similar enterprises all over the world as to be hardly worth describing. Letters were opened and eagerly read but not answered with any great despatch; and in due course they vanished into the yawning mouth of a patent file which meant that we scarcely expected to see them again. Manuscripts had a way of disappearing that struck us at times as uncanny. Often the place would be turned upside down in a mad search for one of these and presently we would come on it staring up at us from a table, where it had so long done duty as a saucer for the teapot or otherwise usefully functioned that we had grown oblivious of its real nature. Spare pulls and ancient galleys, on the other hand, were reverently husbanded for weeks together. Bad writers, we had long since discovered, differ from good by their greater numbers and intense willingness to write, and thus we became masters in the art of defence and evasion. And somehow or other the magazine always appeared on time.

We were as happy and innocent a little band as anywhere could be found and yet we were an object of suspicion in some quarters, both from the ethical and political points of view. Politically, no doubt, we laid ourselves open: in a country where a man could be refused admission to the Labour Party on the grounds that, as a professed liberal, he was too leftwing, it is clearly imprudent to be anything but somewhat to the right of Lord Palmerston. A clerical spy came snooping one day when I was there alone (Peadar would have made short work of him), one of that wretched sort that come sidling up to ask if the other people in the house go to Mass or not: a big burly fellow with purple jowls and the marks of gravy down his waistcoat.

" They say you're all communist in here ! " he growled.

" O Lord, father, what's that you're saying ? " I quavered.

" And materialist ! ! "

" O Lord, father."

" And anti-clerical ! ! ! "

" O Sacred Heart ! " and now there was a ring of such true, such fervent horror and grief in my voice that he was mollified and spent a little time in conversation, extracting from me before he left an undertaking not to believe in leprachauns or fairies. He was very keen on the point, apparently entertaining for these little creatures a dislike as great as for communists and materialists: it may be that he dreaded their competition.

Morally we were under a bit of a cloud from the mere fact of our connexion with literature. In Ireland the Victorian notion prevails that writers, and artists in general, are wonderfully wicked people. A newspaper threatened with litigation by one such miscreant was urged by its lawyer to stand firm, on the ground, it is said, that no Irish jury would find for a painter. And the whole question of morals is one on which the Irish people are abnormally sensitive. An old Dublin story is of how a certain store was asked to remove the pink plaster forms from its window, lest their vague resemblance to the female body should trouble the thoughts and figure in the dreams of masculine passers-by. Pious women have been advised not to use a particular object of feminine hygiene, lest their sensual instincts be momentarily gratified by its insertion: whosever the inspired mind at the back of this counsel, one can only echo the words of Oliver Gogarty's character, the mother of numerous children, who listened for a few moments to a Franciscan preaching on matrimony and left, remarking " I wish to God I knew as little about it as that one."

Nothing is too absurd for them, nothing too far-fetched: they hear the Devil padding after them all the clock round. One day a shop in Dublin came out with a placard advertising " Honey ! Fruit of an Intimate Collaboration between Bee and Flower ! " and the next time I passed by, hoping to savour this once again, the placard had disappeared. This may have been purely fortuitous: on the other hand it may have been in response to a shocked protest. Think of the silliest thing possible in this direction, and you will find it capped and outclassed and left far behind by reality.

For ourselves, under the shadow of this mass psychosis, we

were as proper as could be, and had we ever gone astray the printers would kindly but firmly have led us back to the path: yet the stigma remained and we bore it as best we could, smiling bravely through our tears.

We were greatly helped in all our perplexities by Sean O'Faolain, the first editor of the magazine, whose literary judgement and wise counsel were always at its disposal. Sean stands out in Dublin like a rock in foaming seas. In appearance he is like some respectable English burgher, tall and spare, rosy and blue-eyed; he pulls on a pipe in a calm English way and speaks in a manner imperturbable as it is urbane. He possesses moreover an integrity which is entirely alien to the Irish genius; and his mere presence soothes and reassures. Under it all he is as dotty as they come. He suffers intermittently from violent rushes of blood to the head which bear fruit in the shape of resounding letters to the *Irish Times* ; and I understand that for every one of them that he posts, ten are written and torn up. Perfectly aware that his adversaries are not worth the powder and shot, he falls to and peppers them with a will. On one occasion he proposed to sue a Bishop: and richly as that Bishop deserved to be sued and greatly as we all would have relished the proceedings, there can be no doubt but that it was the dream of a madman. Over the rest of us, however, he had always a wholesome and restraining influence.

But the sweetness and harmony prevailing within that little island were owing, I think, to the character of Peadar in the first place. It is not enough to say, in the hackneyed phrase, that he was a ray of sunshine: he was the sun itself. Very often he nearly drove us mad. Each month, as the editor, it was his duty to write a stirring editorial, a clarion call to the youth of the country to gird up its loins or a spirited denunciation of one of the many things that required denouncing. When the moment for writing it came—or rather when it had already long passed and the telephone calls came from the despairing printer as monotonous and sad as the toll of a funeral bell— he could seldom or never be found. To attempt to pin him down was like trying to pick up a ball of quicksilver between the fingers. He was all over Dublin on a dozen special ploys of his own, every one of them concerned with the welfare of other people. Doggedly as we might track him down to his place of concealment he had always just left it, or else the spoor was an old one: only when at last we gathered glowering round the blank space in the proofs and devised emergency ways of filling it he would bustle in and remark with a delighted chuckle: " And now for the ould editorial ! "

He never allowed the depressing state of affairs in Ireland to weigh on his spirits. He was fully alive to it, of course: a favourite comment of his was, that the young men who formerly came to him with manifestos now only wanted a fiver. But he continued gay and alert, brimming with ideas and hoping for good things round the next corner.

A curious thing about Peadar is that he doesn't drink: curious, because most good Irishmen do, and heavily. I would always recommend caution in dealings with an Irish teetotaler: indeed, a line in a recent play to the effect that there was never a Pioneer but was a bastard at heart, strikes me as one of the weighty utterances in modern Irish writing. Peadar is a most triumphant exception to this rule, and happily, for were his natural ebullience to be heightened by artificial means the rest of us would be worn out. Not every one can hope to keep pace with him as it is.

He is generous, wicked, imaginative and passionately interested in his fellow beings: a man who would never change his tone of voice were he addressing a cardinal or a tramp. If this affectionate tribute has been paid at some length and in what may appear as a rather personal way, it is only because for me he embodies the Ireland that I love.

V

ALL HONOUR TO ST. PATRICK

ONCE upon a time I chanced to be dining in a hotel in a small English town on St. Patrick's Day. A long trestle table had been set up down the middle of the restaurant and round it sat a company of jovial, red-faced, perspiring men, some wearing green paper hats, all with the shamrock in their button-hole. The solid part of the meal was over and the celebrants were settling pously down to the bottle and exercise of wit.

" Buckingham Palace ? Is that a hotel or something ? "

Howls of laughter greeted the quip. Emerald streamers darted hither and thither about the room, wavered and fell in one's plate. From a neighbouring bar came the lusty strains of " The Boys of Wexford " intermingling with those yet farther off of " The Wearing of the Green." Small parties of excited youths were ranging the streets outside, shouting and cheering. Now would come the sound of a sudden fierce altercation: now, again, the tinkle of falling, broken glass.

I observed that the lips of some one at our table were moving.

" What did you say ? " I screamed.

" I said," he bawled, " what on earth must St. Patrick's Day be like in Dublin ? "

Yes, to be sure. I remembered his reasonable inquiry as the day of Ireland's Saint came round again this year.

It began with a cold wet cheerless morning. The wind appeared to blow from all points of the compass at once, a trick of which Dublin winds have the secret. The sky was a grey feathery mass; the rain pattered down in little stinging freezing drops. From some of the public buildings dangled the gold, white and green flag of the Republic, limp and forlorn. The shops were closed, the streets nearly empty, the people at Mass.

At some moment in the morning a pageant of Irish industry began gradually to assemble in St. Stephens Green. Lorries advertising this and that Irish product or activity were slowly easing themselves into their places, causing disruption to the traffic. Sometimes it was a little hard to grasp the idea behind the displays they mounted; for example, a Board na Mona (Turf Board) lorry was transformed into a simple hencoop, protected by wire netting and decorated with flowers in which half a dozen hens ran peevishly up and down. Between these ruffled birds and the highly interesting and important work of the Board it was difficult to see a connexion. Other lorries drew attention to the excellence of certain English goods, toothpaste and cigarettes and so on, of which the makers had opened factories in Ireland and which therefore at a pinch could be included. The truly native products of whiskey and stout were also represented, drawing a faint cheer from the lookers-on.

Later on the newspapers would remark with satisfaction on the great progress made by Irish industry since the founding of the State.

The Anti-Partition League had put its oar in, as was to be expected, and their *tableaux vivants* struck a welcome note of fantasy in the prosaic turn-out. One of these had an Orangeman in bowler hat and sash vainly trying to make his way across a barrier to a tall handsome young man in green while a fat and truculent John Bull prevented him. Another showed Erin in stately green robes and golden crown plucking at the strings of a harp and mourning her six lost counties, which sat huddled together in front of her sniffing loudly and wiping their noses on the backs of their hands. The figure of Robert Emmett stood below a gallows fearlessly confronting a judge in scarlet robes; a placard quoted him to the effect that his epitaph was never to be written until Ireland took her place among the nations of the world and demanded: WHEN?

The public received these inflammatory gestures with calm, if not indifference. Even the children showed no concern for the plight of Robert Emmett but stared glumly in front of them as if their thoughts were elsewhere. Their English contemporaries, faced with a spectacle of the kind would have given delighted cries of " Go on! string 'im up! get on wiv it! " or other such signs of childish interest; but these little souls were speechless and impassive as orientals. A man pushed by with several small girls dressed in blue coats and hats and white socks, with their pigtails tied up in bright red ribbon. On such a day the colour scheme could hardly have been an accident, must surely have been intended as a demonstration, the work of some implacable diehard, but nobody minded.

For that matter, who in Ireland does mind about such things? The Anti-Partition League is always ready with its peep-shows, its leaflets and posters, its denunciatory references to " police states " and " occupied territories." Politicians, without a single constructive idea in their noodles except for their own welfare, can lash a crowd to fury by harping on the injustice of the Border. Americans of Irish descent are fond of raising an easy cheer in the same way and can always depend on space in the newspapers for it: to read some of these newspapers, indeed, you would think the disunity of Ireland was one of Washington's larger worries. Some lone crusader may announce his intention of recruiting and training a private army to invade and conquer the North. Foreigners are button-holed in private conversation and Ireland's case, suitably distorted, is put to them with an intensity of emotion that carries them away: returning home they gravely report that on this issue at least all shades of opinion are in agreement.

There is, however, a gulf between public attitudes and

private opinion in Ireland; it is the land of Double Think and Double Speak. Should any one wish to test the truth of this he need only sit back and quietly watch what is done, ignoring all that is said. It will gradually come to his notice that when all the breast-beating and tub-thumping are over, the sobs hushed and the tears dried, the Irish very coldly and shrewdly do whatever seems to them wise and convenient. They are as canny a race of men as ever walked the earth.

There is another side of this question which ought not to be forgotten. The Border is the last of Ireland's grievances, real and fancied. The mind takes fright at the thought of what will happen when it is gone. From that day on the national pastime of railing at England will have to be given up. A wit has suggested that, on the contrary, then will be the moment to begin work on the most grievous injustice of all—namely, that the sun rises just a little earlier there than here; and on the face of it the problem, being insoluble, seems wonderfully adapted to Irish needs. But too strong a protest against the arrangement might be condemned in certain quarters as contrary to faith and morals. It might be held, after deliberation in conclave, that responsibility for it did not entirely lie with the English. The quarters alluded to have not always been as sensitive to the propriety of national-ist claims as they apparently are to-day; they might once again come heavily down on the side of the established order.

For this reason and others the patriots should be in no hurry to sweep the partition away. There is no urgent need in their soul for the practical benefits of such a move to compare with the urgent need of feeling themselves wronged and of burning John Bull in effigy. They are constantly telling us how ill-adapted they are to this world, how one of their feet only is on the earth and the other in heaven, how alien, helpless and strange they feel in this life, how eagerly they look forward to that beyond the grave. On the evidence it looks as if they might be mistaken: and in any case there is no guarantee whatever that people unable to adapt themselves to this world will not prove an intolerable nuisance in the next one too: in fact, we may reasonably assume that they will. But that is their story and they are holding to it and it hardly squares with the frequent and impassioned demands for the " return " of the Belfast industries.

From their carryings on it might be suspected that the patriots feel this themselves. If the division of Ireland is an injustice, as they say, the task before them is surely to do away with it without creating another. They must induce the people of the North to join them of their own free will. They must persuade these fanatical Protestants that they would really be happier under a regime over which the Church of Rome has an absolute control. They must bring these hardheaded, hard-working, tax-paying, civically-minded creatures to believe that the gay anarchy of the South would suit them very much better. Nothing is impossible, but a programme of this kind would seem to call for an immense and sustained effort. It is so much jollier to strike attitudes and so much more appropriate to the Celtic genius. And hence on every public occasion there are these elaborate charades, staged in the happy confidence that nothing will come of them.

The pipers in their green and saffron kilts now set up a horrid wail, like the wail of a hundred massed banshees, and the procession jogged slowly off in the rain. It took just twenty minutes to pass a given point and it was the highlight of the day. Nothing remained but hurling and football matches in the afternoon and the Dog Show at Ballsbridge. Everything was closed out of respect for the Saint, shops, pubs, places of entertainment. People walked drearily through the wet streets with dull Sunday faces, longing for all to be over. My companion of that evening years ago in England would have found the contrast an instructive one. Could these limp Dubliners have been transferred by magic to Broadway, for example, they too would surely have capered and cut up and cracked skulls in the blithe old tradition. With all the Jews and Italians and Germans looking on they would have become exuberantly and aggressively Irish. There would then have been alien presences, even perhaps hostile ones, against which to react and before which to show off. But alas ! what is the point of being Irish when every one else is Irish too ?

Ennui, which is always just round the corner in Ireland, now openly stalked abroad. But the minutes and hours of the long grey day crept by and brought steadily nearer the hope of release. The brief space of permitted drinking in the hotels loomed closer and closer. Those who had been wise enough to lay in a provision against the saintly drought were already benefiting by their foresight. The spirit of Bacchus stirred uneasily in its sleep.

Some of us went down to the Dolphin in a band, hoping to shake off a little the despondencies of the fiesta. Happy scenes of revelry met the eye the moment we passed within. Unsteady figures cannoned into us, apologizing at once with a fine florid courtesy and sweeping exaggerated bows as we moved towards the Grill. Our path was blocked for a moment or two by a man whom we instantly recognized as one of Dublin's rationalist free-thinkers. He had taken exception to what he described as the " Protestant kind of laugh " of another guest and was offering to fight it out then and there. Laying a hand on one of our shoulders he appealed to us all to recognize the justice of his complaint. His adversary stood beside him and laughed repeatedly, an inane high-pitched laugh in which for the life of us we could detect no sectarian flavour. We passed hurriedly on, knowing that we stood near the brink of something dark and strange.

We made our way through the medley as best we could and sat down at a table. Our neighbour was a plethoric gentleman who sat, head bowed in hands, in front of a double whiskey, fast asleep. Another double whiskey stood at the place opposite him with no one apparently there to drink it. It was a sight of pathos, calling to mind those stories of broken-hearted creatures who celebrate the anniversary of some dear lost one by eating in solitude a dinner served for two. Perhaps some private tragedy was similarly being enacted now? was that libation poured to the memory of some dead hero of the Irish Resistance? or simply one who had fallen victim to the rigours of an earlier St. Patrick's Day? But we looked again and saw that here was no phantom drinker but a man of flesh and blood. It was just that he was kneeling down, his legs under the table, his head on the seat of the chair, unconscious. The waiters were amused and tolerant in the delightful way of their land. For as long as he needed it the amnestied diner could depend on their support and protection. Presently he gurgled and, struggling to rise, rolled over and lay twitching at our feet. The waiters kindly lifted him up and propped him in his chair, whereupon, to their hilarity, he vanished under the table once more.

" Down the well again ! "

" He's gone to look for his boots ! "

And there he lay unheeded yet safe through the evening or, for all we knew, until the cool light of another day broke into the empty room. And the little incident stayed in our minds as a felicitous rounding-off to the whole occasion. Mass in the morning, vacuity through the day, oblivion at night: religion, inertia, alcohol: Ireland's Saint had once more been honoured in the appropriate style. And of the three leaves of the Irish shamrock the kindest and best is alcohol. From all terrors of life and death, from goblins, leprechauns and bishops, from sudden intimations of reality, dear Booze, set us for a moment free ! so perhaps the Invocation in the preamble to the Constitution might be amended.

VI

A FRESH EYE

WITH the first swallows of the year came Mr Bingham-Childs. A friend of us both had sent him along with a letter of introduction, begging me to show him Dublin. On reading it I gave a little whine of self-pity, for the immediate future seemed likely to be full of visits to Guinness's Brewery, the National Museum and other historic edifices in which no resident normally sets foot; but there was no need for anxiety. Mr. Bingham-Childs merely wished to absorb the atmosphere and to meet Dublin intellectuals, of which he understood there were a great number.

He was a young man with a cheerful rosy face and blue untroubled eyes which he fixed unwinkingly upon me as he outlined his views on the Irish situation. Ireland has been explained to me by English visitors more times than I can remember, but the savour of it never grows any less. He had been in the country some forty-eight hours and was bemused with love and admiration. Further, he was obsessed with guilt at the sorrows of Irish history for which he appeared to feel in some way directly responsible. Mr. Bingham-Childs so obviously could never have hurt a fly that I felt bound to intervene at this. Let him forget about Irish history, I urged, for the simple reason that Irish history did not really exist. People who cannot tell you accurately what happened next door last week have no history: they make do instead with legend and myth which are both more amusing and more advantageous.

I described to him a conversation I once had with a

National teacher, over which I ponder to this day. The earnest young man had assured me that one of the great blessings of the English withdrawal from Ireland was that now at last, after centuries of mystification, history could be properly taught in schools. Myth, propaganda, superstition—except that approved by the Church—all had been swept away, and wholesome fact had taken their place. I asked him at what moment in time he would begin the story of this land and he answered, gravely, from when the Phoenicians conquered it by weaving their magic spells.

And for my own part, I told Mr. Bingham-Childs, sorrowfully wagging my head, I had too often watched the events of ordinary life around me gradually assume in reminiscence the colour and the radiance of a folk-tale to read the accounts of things far off with anything but a tranquil and pleasurable disbelief.

" Oh *but* . . . " said Mr. Bingham-Childs.

His voice flowed easily on. I began to fear that as we moved about together he might involve us in awkward scenes. Once I had journeyed late at night from Killiney to Dublin in a crowded bus with a pair of English Mass Observers. The female, who was if anything slightly the more dotty, had been descanting on Irish wrongs and Saxon wickedness in exactly this strain and at the top of a voice that put one in mind of a cockatoo. We were at the rear of the bus; at the front and greatly the better for drink was an old I.R.A. gunman who, maddened by the English accent, presently made his way towards us. An altercation followed, with the I.R.A. man abusing the female Mass Observer for just these wrongs which, from the height of her parlour pinkery, she was so freely deploring. She saw herself as the lately emancipated victim of the same wicked forces as had plagued and tormented and beggared Ireland: he saw her as merely another quacking Saxon. Her sympathies were plainly

modifying themselves as the discussion proceeded; and it
ended, to my mingled joy and terror, with the debauched
veteran falling heavily into her lap.

An evening at the Abbey Theatre seemed a good point
of departure and Mr. Bingham-Childs brightened as the
suggestion was made. He remarked at once that one of his
aims in visiting Dublin was to see at last some really good
plays, after all the tawdry nonsense of the West End of
London. Audiences, he gravely continued, were a factor
of the highest importance too: he should welcome the
opportunity of sitting in one that was really intelligent and
critical. I began to feel as if our positions were reversed and
it was he who was showing me around.

Both the title of the play we saw and the name of its
author escape my memory but it was rich in P.Q. or Peasant
Quality, an attribute hard to define but greatly prized by
the theatre directors. The curtains went up on the dim
smoky interior of a cabin in " the wesht " with an aged crone
huddled over the fire, passing remarks of a typically racy
kind. Ragged figures came and went: a bottle circulated:
there was a struggle. The upshot of it all, as I remember,
was that somebody got the better of somebody else.

Mr. Bingham-Childs greatly enjoyed the whole thing. A
nice thing about the true-blue English visitor is that he not
only approaches the Abbey expecting to see a worth-while
play but leaves it convinced that he has done so. In the
intervals we repaired to a neighbouring bar where we fell in
with a jovial stranger who explained that England's wars had
all been won, as her literature had been written, by Irishmen;
with which my companion fully agreed. He stood erect with
shining eyes for " The Soldier's Song " at the end of the
performance. He was a little disappointed to learn that
Dublin could offer nothing in the way of a nocturnal life. He
had expected apparently to find some kind of an Irish

Montparnasse along the banks of the Liffey with a row of brightly lit cafés where the wit flashed back and forth in perpetual scintillation. But such was his equable and unassuming nature that he accepted a Milk Shake in one of the ice cream parlours along O'Connell Street, all that the city could offer at that hour, without a word of reproach.

My services were not to be required on the following day as he was beginning his round of the Dublin intelligentsia. He had made an appointment for coffee at eleven o'clock with a man whose distinguished name was so familiar to me that when at eleven-thirty a plaintive voice inquired for me on the telephone I was not in the least surprised.

" He said the Oriental Café in Grafton Street," the voice explained. " I suppose I *am* in the right place ? "

He gave details of his position and I assured him there was no mistake.

" That's all right, then," said the voice with relief in it.

At ten minutes past twelve it was back again, subdued and flattened, and asked what I was doing for lunch. Nothing, I said, and we made an appointment for half past one. Then I leaned back in my chair and fell into a meditation. Is there anything truly wrong in the little harmless white lies that bring peace and joy to honest men ? Mr. Bingham-Childs had sounded full of the dejection of a nice child whose toy has been snatched from its hand. His pleasure in Dublin ought not to be spoiled for want of a word from me. I picked up the telephone and, having got through to Davy Byrnes, inquired if by any chance the missing intellectual were on the premises. By a coincidence he was; and I begged him to tell me if he happened to know the whereabouts of a Mr. Bingham-Childs.

" He's here incognito, scouting for the B.B.C.," I said. " Mind you, I've said nothing."

A silence followed these words during which the very wire seemed to be vibrating with emotion.

" Did you say the B.B.C. ? " the intellectual presently asked, with a suspicion of hoarseness in his voice.

" That's it. Only he doesn't want it to leak out. He believes he will get a better idea of who's who in Irish culture by informal contact. Or so I hear."

There was another silence.

" Well, if I come across him I'll let you know," said the intellectual, casually. " I don't think much of the B.B.C. myself, as you know, but I should like to be of assistance."

Twenty minutes later Mr. Bingham-Childs telephoned in high feather to say there had been a mix-up and would I think him very rude if he suggested our lunching some other day.

" His American agent had cabled urgently for an essay," said Mr. Bingham-Childs in awed tones. " He hadn't even the time to put me off. All he could do was hurl himself at his typewriter and compose."

" Much of the best work gets done that way," I said. " Would you mind not telling him that you've been in touch with me ? "

" Why ever not ? "

" In this part of the world it is better when the left hand doesn't know what the right hand is up to."

" *O how delightfully odd.*"

Nothing more was seen of him in the next days: serenely he had plunged into the uncharted morass of Dublin cultural life, supported only by faith and innocence. News trickled in: he had lunched here, dined there, boozed up somewhere else: he had been seen to purchase a copy of *The Face and Mind of Ireland* by Mr. Arland Ussher: he was said to have been invited—and the rumour set my mind at rest completely—to the home of a celebrated literary lawyer.

I was impatient to learn what he was making of it all. For all his candour he gave the impression of being nobody's fool and at some moment the salient fact of Irish letters to-day must surely catch his eye: that in Ireland there are dozens of brilliant writers and few, quite remarkably few, manuscripts. The Englishman assumes that the existence of the first will lead to the production of the second, an attitude which reveals the gulf between English and Irish modes of thought. The Irishman deplores this vulgar insistence on achievement. He feels that it is a splendid thing to be a writer and that little or nothing is added to it by writing: even, indeed, that it might be a grave mistake.

There are of course modern Irish writers, and fine ones, who have so far broken with custom as to produce books; but they are not a patch on the others. And they have put their cards on the table, the last thing a man should do if he wants to keep a reputation in Dublin. It is all very well to fulminate briefly against every one and everything in the pages of an obscure and short-lived magazine from time to time. You can dismiss the Victorians or the Russians in a paragraph, you can in your haphazard little review describe *The Times Literary Supplement* as " semi-literate " and still leave your own mysterious potentialities intact: you will be reverently quoted by members of your own coterie in further short papers and savagely assailed by the others and it is all great fun; but once you put pen to paper at length and for years on end you give the game away and expose yourself to withering blasts of scorn.

Other, graver snags lie in the path of the Irish writer. There is the difficulty of finding new subjects in a small empty country where everything seems to have been chewed over and over again to the point of nausea. There is the censorship and behind the censorship the hosts of wavering, impure minds that acquiesce in it and make it possible. It is in fact that horrid mentality, and not the small committee that sits in Dublin gravely adding title after title to an already fantastic list, that kills literature. A young man may produce a book that is perfectly honest and fresh and sincere and some pious yahoo may get hold of it, read it with but a partial understanding, mark a few passages that he deems perilous to faith and morals—of which he very likely has neither—and forward it with zeal to the censors. The words "banned in Ireland" are something of a joke abroad but it is not so easy to smile them away at home. There may be social unpleasantness and repercussions in business affairs for the author; and in any case his natural and proper audience has gone. It is true that banned books can be ordered directly from England and will in all likelihood come safely through the Customs, but that is possible only to people with the means and, as it were, in the know: there is a touch of the black market about it. Such books will not be found in Irish bookshops or in public libraries; and they will be read by the wrong people for the wrong reasons, passed lovingly and furtively from hand to hand like those treasured copies of muck-raking Sunday newspapers that Irish servant girls in England send home to their fathers, hidden away in the leaves of the *Catholic Herald*.

The first unexpected brush with that rancid Irish puritanism, that fear and hatred of life, is a bitterly wounding experience and one that may even sour a new talent into silence. And if the young author tries again one of two things may happen, both detrimental. He can give in and work his passage back to respectability by saying what he doesn't mean. Or he can "give them something to bloody well ban me for" which is another way of saying what he doesn't mean and so of spoiling his work. In the latter case his public henceforward will be mainly English and American, that is to say, cannot really know what he is talking about; and there is a danger of his ending up as a buffoon or a whimsical or a purveyor of " Oirish " charm. The most difficult thing for an Irish writer to do is to go calmly on and say what he wants to say without troubling himself as to whom it will please or annoy.

This has all been noted before, of course, and will be noted again at frequent intervals for centuries to come.

Mr. Bingham-Childs telephoned again: he had just been talking to the Irish La Rochefoucauld.

"Such wit ! A mind like a rapier ! If his books are anything like his conversation . . ."

" He hasn't written any."

" No ? Really ? How extraordinary. Teeming with ideas . . . so refreshing . . . some of his conceptions are amazing. He said the universe will come to an end presently because no one will believe in it any longer. Or stop, was it that ? No, hang it, I've got it wrong. But he had me spellbound . . . spellbound . . ."

In the evening he telephoned again to say that in his opinion Dublin was the Athens of the modern world. From then on indeed he telephoned every day afresh, bubbling over with the joy of his discoveries: and with each preposterous statement I was able to stick another little flag mentally on the map of the battlefield.

One of the things that he may have enjoyed the most, as an utter change from the sober intellectual habits of his own country was the note of positive affirmation. It is to be met with not only in Dublin but through the whole of Ireland, is indeed one of the strongest and happiest of Irish attributes. The newspapers breathe it out in great rosy puffs: the clergy fan it on every possible occasion: among the nationalists it rises to a pitch that leaves one speechless with wonder. For instance, you may read in a pamphlet advocating the spread of the Irish language and the boycott of English books and

papers that the Gaelic culture is the supreme achievement of
Europe. Many of us will be on delicate ground here, for we
may not be as familiar with Gaelic culture as, evidently, we
ought to be. We shall no doubt have heard the language
spoken at odd times: the occasional careful halting speech in
the Dáil, a gossip in a bus between two Christian Brothers
carried on with a maximum of self-consciousness and—as
one Gaelic scholar avers—a minimum of proper syntax, or
the rough talk of peasants in the west. "Patois rauque,
exhumé du fonds des siècles," wrote a Frenchman after an
experience of the kind, but that is simply the view of one man.
Not all of us are qualified to consider the claim of the militant
Gael nor to weigh his culture against that of Greece or Rome,
of mediaeval Christendom or the Italy of the Renaissance.
And certain special obstacles often lie in the way of any one
attempting to do so. Once I read, in no nationalist leaflet
but a restrained and judicious textbook, that the old Irish
music was the finest and sweetest in the world and, old
melomaniac that I am, pricked up my ears in joyous antici-
pation: but they dropped again at once. "Unfortunately,"
the writer went on to say, "not a single note of it has been
preserved." There would be nothing for it but to accept the
supremacy of Irish music by faith, as clearly the writer had
done, but this is possible only for certain types of mind. All
this is not to the point, however; our ignorance, our doubts,
our hesitations are neither here nor there: the beauty of the
thing and the special grace of this fiery Gael lie in the fact
that he is as unaware of the other elements in European
culture as we of his and yet, simply and superbly, he arranges
them in their order of precedence.

And here perhaps a tribute should be paid to the liberating
influence of the Catholic education. The other side of the
picture is only too familiar: the repression, the cramping
effect of dogma, the staleness created in men's minds when

they feel themselves in possession of the final and absolute truth. Yet the Catholic enjoys a mental freedom unknown to members of other sects and, above all, to those who describe themselves as free-thinkers. From his childhood he has been wont to accept without examination statements that on the face of them are absurd. His mind is free from those habits of scrutiny and analysis which shackle the brains of other men. When therefore the patriot utters his declaration on Irish music or Gaelic culture: or if an eminent ecclesiastic should state, not as a matter of conjecture but of fact, that the Virgin Mary was five foot seven inches, weighed seven stone, had blue eyes and hair that was a " class of mahogany": he is simply offering a truth which has been revealed to him and he would as soon think of arguing it out with a sceptic with all the tedious concomitants of fact and figure as he would of questioning the infallibility of the Pope.

When Mr. Bingham-Childs telephoned next, I asked if he was ever likely to have an evening free.

" Oh yes: I've seen much less of you than I should have liked. But you do understand? This has been such a wonderful experience . . . welcomed everywhere . . . never thought it possible . . ."

" I want to take you to the Pearl Bar. It's where the cream of Dublin intelligence assembles. You can see them all together at once."

" And you know them all? " cried the eager voice.

" More or less."

" Ah ! "

The lounge of the Pearl Bar was not yet very full as we climbed up to it the following evening. It looked indeed fuller than it was, owing to the presence of the editor of the *Irish Times*. This huge gentleman possessed the gift not only of creating by himself the sense of a party but of bestowing on the whole bar a distinguishing air: without him, it became something quite different. Vast, genial, he would sit there by the hour, his comfortable frame shaking with laughter at the sallies of his companions, and draw sagely at his pipe; but should one enter whom he really wished to avoid this seemingly inert, apparently rooted, mass would suddenly vanish, now here, now gone, with the amazing finality of a Bodily Assumption.

" Who's that ? " whispered Mr. Bingham-Childs.

No introduction could be made for the moment since, near the large friendly editor, sat another of a different kind. His paper was the most widely read and perhaps the sourest of all the Catholic publications in Ireland. Moral reprobation was a feature of it; and once indeed I had been mildly vexed to find myself described in it by a clerical gentleman as " a mouth spewing obscenity and blasphemy." The worthy cleric, who was no doubt of a practical rather than a literary bent, had failed to grasp the point of something I had written and was unable to contain himself. To me it seemed that the little episode released us from all mutual social obligations, a view which the editor, to judge from his effusiveness on the sole occasion that I was trapped into meeting him, did not share. Nor was it in fact a properly Dublin view. There is a peculiar frivolity about the whole of life in Dublin; nothing matters, nothing is serious, least of all what any one thinks or says. And this is perhaps as it should be, since no one thinks what he says or says what he thinks. It was suggested to me, for that matter, in defence of this individual that he possibly never meant what he said or allowed to be published. A lively discussion had followed as to whether this would make him worse or better, and ended inconclusively.

I steered Mr. Bingham-Childs to a table, avoiding corners—one should never let oneself be cornered in the Pearl—and choosing a site from which a fast retreat would be possible and which yet afforded a wide view of the room.

One of Dublin's major poets immediately joined us, with a thirsty look on his face. He was glad to depend on our kindness that evening because the confidence he felt in certain racehorses had turned out to have been misplaced. This in no way reflected on his judgement: as a wise old lady once observed, in Irish racing the things to consider are the owner, the jockey and the horse and you need to know what is passing in the minds of all three before you lay down a shilling. Yet the pain of the loss itself had cast a shadow over his mind and he launched, in his beautiful voice, a diatribe against Ireland and all her works, her passion for mediocrity, her crucifixion of genius: he lamented the passing of his best years among marshmen and Firbolgs: he threatened to shake the dust of her off his feet and to seek his living henceforward in strange places among foreign men.

Mr. Bingham-Childs murmured something about oases of Christian culture in a world distracted by materialism and the voice was hushed and over the craggy peasant face stole a look of infinite compassion. Its owner applied himself without uttering again to his Guinness as being of its own nature permanently and unassailably good and left as soon as he had finished it.

An unknown young man came up and waved a wad of grimy paper at us.

" I've written a pome," he remarked. " Will I read it ? "

" By all means," said Mr. Bingham-Childs, companionably. I began almost to wish he had been the more usual kind of tourist.

" But you will sign me up ? " proceeded the youth.

" I beg your pardon ? "

" Sign me up. The way you signed **** up. Didn't you sign **** up ? "

" I haven't signed any one up. I don't think I know what you mean."

" Then isn't he the biggest bloody liar in the world ? " and the stranger flounced indignantly away.

Seeing myself poised, as so often before, on the brink of exposure I began hurriedly to explain what might have been in the poet's mind. The word of my friend's presence was sure to have gone round Dublin and it was likely that some people might have put a wrong construction on his interest in cultural affairs. The belief that in Ireland a rich vein of talent was waiting to be opened up was very persistent abroad, and publishers and agents were in the habit of coming over in relays to scout for themselves. They would stay a week or so and leave delightedly, fed with promises of dramas, poems, novels and brilliant new interpretations of James Joyce. Perhaps it had been assumed that Mr. Bingham-Childs was one of them ? since a pure disinterested love of Irish letters was new in Dublin experience. If so, I urged, the thing to do was to play up in order not to cause disappointment and give offence: did he agree ?

To my relief Mr. Bingham-Childs, laughing merrily, agreed. Yet even as he laughed there was a gleam in his eye that was not of pure amusement, or rather it was of an amusement extended some little way beyond the immediate joke and, therefore, disquieting. One of the many articles of Irish faith to which I have never subscribed is that all Englishmen are very very simple. I had seen that gleam in English eyes before and most often indeed as they rested on an Irish object.

The familiars of the Pearl were making their appearance one by one. In trotted a gnome with a face like a bottom and his hair *en brosse*, celebrated even in Dublin for the malignant venom of his attacks on all and sundry. Next came an Anglo-Irishman of letters with a mad light in his pale eyes, carrying with an air of decision and importance a briefcase that bulged with sandwiches and pyjamas. A literary editor with an air of gentle, refined melancholy about him. More poets. Some playwrights. Lawyers. One gaolbird. Civil Servants. Some of this crowd showed signs of incipient persecution mania, due to their having in fact at one time or another been persecuted. A drunk reeled from one table to the next trying to find some one who would listen once more to the tale of an ancient wrong. A little haze of cigarette smoke settled over the room. The bar boys ran hither and thither with their trays like men distracted.

Gradually, imperceptibly, yet steadily, a tide was flowing our way. My companion seemed to possess a kind of lunar attraction. People I barely knew strolled up and complained that it was a long time since we had met. Drinks were bought in a freehanded style unparalleled in my memory. Invitations to lunch and dinner were issued for any day, any time, and with the proviso that my nice English friend should come as well. It was in the nature of a small triumph.

I became engrossed for some little time in an anecdote, muttered by a neighbour into my ear, concerning the Archbishop of Dublin and when I turned back to the party as a whole it was to find that Mr. Bingham-Childs was throwing himself into the game with an abandon of which one would have supposed him incapable. He was, if not by Dublin standards drunk, noticeably elated; and with a splendid lunatic gravity was dishing out contracts right and left. In nothing did he reveal his subtlety, equally unsuspected heretofore, so much as in the fact that he left the exact nature and scope of these contracts undefined. Each of his victims clearly believed himself to have been " signed up "; yet at no moment did Mr. Bingham-Childs make any concrete proposal or volunteer any information as to whom he was allegedly representing. It was a masterpiece, a *tour de force*: it proved once again that when an Englishman puts his mind to it he can be more wickedly Irish than

anything that ever came out of Ireland: and at the end of
the evening, as the lights went up and down and the cries
of " Now, gentlemen, please ! " grew even more urgent, the
honest blue eyes were wide and calm as before.

Humbled, as we all must be in the presence of a master,
I crept through the dark streets at his side. The following
day was to be his last among us: we therefore took leave of
each other.

" I only wish I could have done more to enliven your
stay," I told him.

" But you did a great deal, a great deal ! more than I
had any right to expect," he cried, expansively.

Then he gave a deprecating little giggle.

" I may be silly, you know, but I'm conscious ! "

It was precisely as I had feared, all the way along.

VII

ANY FISH RISING?

THE lilac on the wall turned grey and then brown. The garden wore a drab sulky look as if emphasizing that nothing more was to be expected of it until the roses opened in summer. The sands of life ran low. Almost anywhere in Ireland, except possibly Mullingar, seemed more inviting than Dublin. I began to fancy that I was suffering from some rare disease and telephoned to a specialist for an appointment; but his secretary answered that he was away at Lough Corrib.

" They are waiting on the mayfly," she said. " Surely you must have known that ? "

The surprise in her voice brought me at once down to earth. Caught up in the trivia of everyday things I had failed to notice the approach of one of the serious events in the Irish year. All over the country now hawk eyes were fixed on lake and stream, razor-like minds weighed the chances of this season against the last. In whole villages hardly a tap of work would be done till the magic fortnight was over. In dark pools and gold-ribbed shallows the crafty trout were biding their time and considering how best to make fools of the entire population.

I rushed out and boarded a bus for County ———. Some hours later I arrived at a hotel on the shores of a lake, where the proprietress looked me up and down in a friendly attempt at classification.

" A lunatic ? " she queried. " The place is full of them. Fishing lunatics now. Shooting lunatics in the autumn, Golfing lunatics the whole year round. I bear with them all."

It was a portrait, in the fewest words, of a life. Having uttered it at lightning speed she darted away, her wide straw hat pinned on askew, to greet another batch of lunatics. Three solid men with wine-coloured faces had just come in; each carried a fishing-rod and a basket, each had gay little flies stuck in the brim of his cream linen hat. One was called Guffy, the second was Tabs, and the third was the Major; and the mysterious thing about the trio was that as long as they kept together you could just tell them apart but did one of them become momentarily detached from the others for the life of you you couldn't say which it was. On each big face at present was an expression of wonder and pain.

" Nothing doing," said the Major.

" Blighters are shy," said Tabs.

" The fishing has gone to pot," said Guffy, and the others growled their agreement.

" You'll feel better after your tea," said the proprietress, in the soothing voice she kept for her lunatics. " What'll I give you ? "

The trinity thought it over and gloomily decided for bacon and eggs.

Down by the lake an assortment of people watched and waited. A biting wind was blowing from the east but they paid no attention. From time to time derisive remarks were exchanged about a boatload of duffers drifting helpless before the breeze, their untrammelled lines caught and crissed and crossed in a frenzy of incompetence: otherwise the silence was unbroken. The falling sun touched the tree-tops with gold, the bluebells burned in the shadow of the wood, the distant hills swam in a pearly evening mist, but there were no eyes for anything but the choppy leaden waters of the lake.

A fallen tree protruded over the water and on the extreme tip of its trunk a boy was spread-eagled, his boots waving in air, his congested cheeks an inch or so from the surface. And all at once this urchin raised himself on one arm and howled at the sky: THEY ARE COMING UP! Half a dozen men scrambled eagerly on to the tree, which sank at once beneath their weight and plunged them into the water. A commotion broke out among the watchers on dry land. The policeman leapt on his bicycle and rode away, returning presently with a rod. Alerted, the people of the village came streaming down to the water-side in their twos and threes: and finally in their wake came Guffy and Tabs and the Major, wreathed in smiles, their trousers twinkling as they ran.

Was this boy by any chance a *saboteur*? Had he, in this quiet corner of Ireland, somehow been infected with the spirit of wantonness now sweeping the world? that spirit to which nothing whatever is sacred? For his assertion proved to be wholly unfounded. Nothing came up, no mayfly, still less any trout. Gradually as night approached the murmuring people fell away and at last only the Major and Tabs and Guffy were left, to cast and cast and cast again, their purple faces glowing above the sullen wavelets like three Japanese lanterns, their arms flailing the dusk like the arms of a windmill.

The same thing happened next day and the next and the next. Not a fish was caught or seen. Then the proprietress came to me and spoke as woman to woman. It was clear that something was going on in the locality that was new in human experience. She had telephoned to various parts of Ireland and learned that times had never been better. The three frustrated fishermen sat in the bar every night until long after hours drinking dark brown whiskey and communicating their silent despair to every one else. Their reason, always a delicate thing where trout were concerned, now tottered towards collapse. Remarks were beginning to pass. The hotel business would suffer. Even now the sight of those

three mournful pans entering a room was sufficient to clear
it; and the woe that was written on them affected her own
health and spirits.

" So would you ever go here and there and find out the
cause of it all ? " she implored me. " Sure, they're all three
men of the world. If we can give them some reasonable
explanation they'll move on to another place like sensible
fellows. But this is murder."

I promised to spare no pains to solve the mystery. I
unpacked my notebook, half full as it already was of authentic
misinformation, and sharpened a pencil. To bring peace to
those suffering minds would be a splendid achievement,
comparable in its way to the relief of a starving city. They
should suffer no more for want of assistance from me.

" We've the man for you ! " the people cried, as I
started on my inquiry.

It seemed there was a local genius who was so mad for
the fishing that he had gone on to writing books and lecturing
at the universities and was grown so learned that scholars
came from far and wide to sit at his feet.

" He'll tell you the truth, if any one can ! " they assured me.

The drawback was that I could discover neither his name
nor his whereabouts, although there was a persistent rumour
that he owned a fish shop in Dublin and was probably
minding it.

I wished them all a good morning and went a little farther
down the street. In one of the village shops there resided a
delightful character with a wide, white grin and blue eyes
that blazed with passion as he expounded his favourite theme.
He wore all day long a checked cloth cap with flies stuck over
it in preparedness and fishing-rods were propped in rows
against the walls of his rooms. In his spare time he was a
draper and clothier and ever and anon, against a background
of corduroy trousers, he would launch into a brilliant

harangue on the habits of trout, the life-cycle of the mayfly
and the geological composition of all the lakes of Ireland.
Distractedly from time to time as a customer entered he
would pause and hand him out a pair of trousers or a length
of tweed, waving his money aside the sooner to return to
serious matters.

I could not have come to a better place. Hardly was the
question of the lake raised than he broke into a torrent of
words. He refused to hear a word against the local trout.
In a general sort of way trout had their failings and their
caprices, but a specific complaint of the local trout he was
not prepared to countenance. It was the peculiarly biting
east wind that year was to blame. He would ask me to try
and put myself in the shoes of the trout. Would I not feel
inclined, with a wind scalding the surface like that, to remain
at the bottom where I was comfortably off? It was a
reasonable, a prudent course to pursue and the local trout
were nothing if they were not reasonable and prudent. Those
who held otherwise, who sought more complicated reasons,
more sinister motives for the trout's behaviour merely exposed
their own ignorance and lack of imagination.

So it was as simple as that! He carried me with him
entirely. And there was a real pleasure in talking the thing
out with him. Sport is the one thing in Ireland that people
consider freely and frankly: business, religion and politics
are obscured in mists of evasion: it is only when a horse or
a fish or a bird is under discussion that words are used as a
means of communication rather than as a device for concealment. The statement that I had just heard, precise as
to fact and fearless as to opinion, was like a breath of fresh air.

But I would leave nothing to chance: I would take a
second opinion. Always before my inward eye hung the
stricken faces of Guffy and Tabs and the Major. At the
farther end of the village another famous fisherman had his

workshop: I found him just locking it up for the day and
sallying forth, fully equipped, for a day of sport.

He waited with the utmost good manners and patience
while I explained the nature of my inquiry and the progress
made in it so far. But when the draper's theory was put to
him, he flatly contradicted it. He had been fishing a stretch
for the past seven days that was every bit as vexed with the
wind as the lake, and his basket was full every evening of
two, three and four pounders. If it was all the same to me he
did not propose to divulge the whereabouts of his stretch.
Once it got known the crowds would be after it. But as far
as the wind affecting the fish in the lake was concerned, I
could put it right out of my mind.

Wholly convinced, I begged him to tell me the real cause
of the trouble. A look of infinite knowingness crossed his face.
He glanced up the road to the left and he glanced up the
road to the right and at last, approaching his lips to my
ear, he muttered: " Because there's no trout in that lake
at all ! "

The facts that he went on to reveal, still in that same
hoarse undertone, were enough to chill the blood. During the
war two individuals—if I was agreeable, he proposed to leave
them unnamed—received permission to fish with lines for eel.
But when night had fallen they would creep out and privily
fish with nets for the trout: in no time at all they had the
place cleared. The owner finally noticed this and, while no
remarks were passed, he gave the matter attention, but too
late. There wasn't a trout pulled out of there since, never
mind what any one said. The owner of the fishing rights was
down on the shore every day, eating his heart out, brooding
over the past. I should have a tactful word with him and get
the story confirmed. Mind you, he'd said nothing at all and
he'd be glad enough for his name to be left out of it.

He went on to describe with a wealth of colourful detail

the exact point of the lake where the crime had taken place.
I went there at once and found all just as he had said. There
was the neck of water narrow enough for the extending of
nets from shore to shore: the clump of bushes, so convenient
for hiding a criminal on a moonlight night: the creek, where
a small boat might lie for ever concealed: and the alley
leading up from the creek to the road, where a van could
wait to drive the stolen cargo away through the darkness
to a destination unknown. I stood there appalled at the
fiendish ingenuity of man.

My informant had described the owner of the fishing
rights with the painstaking accuracy he brought to all that
he said, and there was no difficulty at all in picking him out.
He was a bald, fat, melancholy man, dressed in vaguely
nautical attire, who sat on a wooden chair and gazed at the
water in a glum sort of way. So still was he that he seemed a
part of the landscape, but when I broached the affair of the
stolen fish he started as if I had pricked him. He put back
his head and bayed like a dog.

God be with the days when there were fishermen in
Ireland! Why, the lough was simply teeming with trout.
All that was needed was the skill to bring them out. No one
had it now, and it was the custom to blame the fish and the
weather and the flies and, for all he knew, the Government.
It was true all right that two men had once gone around with
tales against the fishers for eel. A watch had been kept and
nets indeed were found, but to whom did they belong? Why,
to these two same informers! Now, wouldn't that make a
dog strike his father?

Here, surely, must be the plain unvarnished truth. The
story held together quite apart from the passionate sincerity
with which it was uttered. And who, after all, was better
placed to know the fishing possibilities of a lake than the
owner of them? I sat down on the shore with my notebook

to compare and collate and sift the evidence. Presently the draper came trotting by, rod on shoulder, and flashed a dazzling grin. Cautiously, for no man likes to hear his considered opinion challenged, I laid before him this new and seemingly unanswerable proposition.

" Don't mind him ! " the expert cried, indignantly. " The owner, is it ? Sure, he's only a friend of the owner's cousin ! An utter stranger ! There's fish in the lake all right but the wind has them beaten ! It's the wind, I'm telling you ! "

I closed my notebook then and returned to the hotel for lunch and a rest. The proprietress was at the front door arguing with a shaggy individual who carried a basket over his arm.

" Look at them, will you, the little lovely things," he was saying. Inside the basket were a row of gleaming trout, freshly gutted, about a pound and a half each one. " You'll not see finer trout than those now," he went on, " and caught no later than this morning."

" Who caught them ? and where ? " the proprietress demanded.

" You'd never ask me to give away the secrets of the trade ? " asked the vendor in shocked tones, looking at her sideways.

" And you'd never charge me eighteenpence apiece for my own trout, I suppose ? " riposted the lady.

" Ah, g'wan out of that, Missus ! "

As God was his eternal judge, he explained, the only obstacle in the way of his providing her with a full and truthful account of how he came by the fish was the inquisitiveness of the local water baillies and the difficulty experienced by honest men these days in keeping body and soul together. One thing he would say and—with a horrible leer—did: the spot where he'd caught them was not a hundred miles from where the ladies were standing. Might he never do a

day's good again if he would stoop to poaching the waters of
a grand woman like Herself: and might the blessed saints in
Heaven take careful note of this prayer and hold him to it.

The flow of words was only cut short when money
changed hands. We carried the little corpses indoors and
examined them closely.

" They are mine ! They are mine all right ! I'd know
them anywhere ! " the proprietress said, ruefully. " I could
have whipped them out of the stream myself from the
bedroom window ! "

Or had they come from the lake ? O complex Irish life ! We
now discussed the question of whether Guffy and Tabs and
the Major should be given trout for their luncheon. Would
the effect of it be to solace and sustain, to bring a reminder
that there still were trout in the world and not so wonderfully
far away ? or would it merely open their wounds afresh ?
even perhaps be interpreted by them, in the present raw
state of their nerves, as a subtle gibe at their lack of success ?
We decided the risk could not be taken. The trout was fed to
the cats lest the smell of it grilling should reach the trinity's
nostrils and possibly drive it mad. The usual lumps of
bleeding steak, wreathed with fried onions, were prepared.
To-day they returned to the kitchen untasted. The position
was growing desperate. Something of the pitiful tenderness
of a mother with an ailing child showed in the face of the
proprietress as she waylaid me outside the dining-room.

" Did you find anything out at all ? " she whispered.

" Oh, I'm making progress, making progress," I assured
her, tapping my notebook.

" Wait till I tell you," she murmured. " There's an old
fellow now that they call Mickey. He's the king of them all
when it comes to sport. He'll give you the truth of it. You'll
find him in the pub below, especially out of hours. This can't
go on any longer. They're going to play at the dominoes now ! "

The pub was just after closing for the Holy Hour as I came up to it and entry could only be gained by a subterfuge. But there sat old Mickey alone in the taproom, with a phalanx of bottles of stout on the window-sill at his elbow. As I came in he pulled the curtains across them, no doubt as a mark of respect for the law. His small bright eyes wavered from me to these curtains as I laid our troubles before him.

"Fishing is the pearl of sports, all right," he remarked gravely. "With a bird, bang! it's over. With a fish, and him on the hook, you've play for a good half-hour. Now isn't that common sense?"

"But there are no fish on the hooks! Isn't that what I'm telling you?"

"Ah well, that's another story."

He thoughtfully drained his glass and sucked the little beads of stout off the ends of his moustache.

"And what's the reason for it?"

"Reason? Now, there's a reason for everything under the sun." He reached for another bottle and poured it out with a swift, practised hand leaving half an inch of foam on the top of the glass and no more. A restful silence fell on the room as he slowly drank it down.

"Tell the gentlemen to study the Scriptures," he said, all at once.

"And the Prophecies of Columcille," he added.

There was a pause for further refreshment. The swimming sensation in the head, familiar to all who search for the truth in Ireland, was gently beginning in mine. Old Mickey finished his bottle and began to speak in level tones and with a quiet final authority that left no room for discussion.

We had only to study the writings mentioned, he said, and we should understand the position at once. We had only to look around us and their teachings would be fully borne out. Armageddon was fast approaching, being preceded by two great wars and any number of minor portents. Of these, the erratic behaviour of the local trout was merely one. Now wasn't that plain common sense and logic?

" Mind you, I was a great sportsman too in my day," said Mickey: " but now " said he, reaching again to the window-sill, " we must all prepare for the end of the world."

And at this the swimming sensation referred to grew to a mighty whirl. Before he had even finished speaking I knew that my brain would be curdled for the rest of the day. I dragged myself out of the room and out of the pub. I stood on the shore of the lake staring wildly about me. The sunlight sparkled on the water like the glint of amusement in a subversive eye. As far as I was concerned the lake should guard its secret for ever.

VIII

"WE ALL WERE LIBELLED!"

ONE of these days a qualified person should write an analysis of the Irish attitude to the law. It is an attitude essentially sound and often attractive but one which contains a singular paradox. As is well known, the Irish have no respect at all for the law as such: one might go further and say they have no real conception of it. The reason sometimes put forward for this is that Law was for centuries associated in their minds with the alien conqueror and thereby came into disrepute. I think it is nearer the truth to say that being wholly governed by Custom, they find an irrelevance in anything else. The forms and procedures are duly observed: the laws of the land are properly framed and established and, no doubt, read very nicely: and the whole is interpreted and applied in a carefree spirit of hit-or-miss such as one would expect rather to find in the Balkans.

The strength and weakness of the system, if system it may be called, is the room that it leaves to considerations other than legal. I believe it may truly be claimed that humanity plays a larger part in decisions here. On the other hand, the Irish notions of equity are so peculiar as to call for a new and distinguishing name. Rich foreigners, for example, would do well to approach an Irish Court with a wary step. A few years ago a wealthy English lady was soaked with a gay impudence which irresistibly called to mind the exploits of Robin Hood. The damages awarded the separate plaintiffs were such that it seemed as if Heaven itself were intervening when one of them fell dead before the sum was paid over.

Reading the reports of it afterwards one could almost hear a ghostly smacking, as of jurors' lips. No one with whom I discussed this affair showed the slightest trace of embarrassment. The general feeling appeared to be, it was fair enough: and wasn't it well for them to be getting the bit of money? and the woman had plenty more, had she not? she'd never miss it! The function of the Court, it was apparently held, was not to arrive at an appropriate conclusion but to undertake a redistribution of wealth. The point of view can perhaps be defended: and that it *was* well for the surviving plaintiff, who shall deny?

The paradox is that, while sceptical of the law and even more so of those who carry it out, the Irish are unusually eager to have recourse to it. They fly to court with the readiness of Indians, or of Englishmen of the Tudor period. It is quite remarkable how many people embark on legal adventures in Ireland: still more so, the pretexts on which these actions arise. This might be explained by the satisfaction it gives to both the national love of a to-do and the national desire for revenge; and yet it is curious that satisfaction should be found in this way, and not in others more adapted to the national genius.

Libel actions are especially plentiful, which need amaze no one. The libel laws of Ireland, as of England, are an open invitation to truffle-hunters at any time; and in Ireland there is a further stimulus provided by certain of the national characteristics. One of these is what often appears to the world at large as an inordinate vanity, but which may more truly be called a desire to preserve " face." An Irishman held up to ridicule suffers in the way that an oriental does; he receives an intimate, piercing wound that by some means or other will have to be made whole. At the same time he possesses a talent for irony and invective which clamours for expression at the expense of other Irishmen who, unhappily, have also their "face" to consider. These two opposing tendencies, playing one on the other, handsomely swell the volume of litigation.

One group in Ireland has discovered a new and wholly ingenious use for the libel laws, namely, the clergy. The gentlemen in black are highly sensitive to criticism and do all in their power to ensure that it never sees the light of day. They have set up a censorship-by-threat-of-proceedings. At the first breath of adverse comment they roar that they are being held up to ridicule and contempt. The line they take as a rule is, first, that they never did what they are alleged to have done. With a bland, almost a papal, assurance they issue denials of incidents that have taken place in public and to the knowledge of hundreds of people. Secondly, they point out that anyway the Bishop told them to do it and they have to obey the Bishop. The Bishop supports them, indeed often pricks them on in the first place.

I should love to give details of some of the choicer examples of this but we should have the heroes of them after us, seeking further and better damages. I once came on an editor in a condition of utter bewilderment over a writ that had just been served.

" He says the event we described never took place ! " the editor was groaning. " But my reporter was there, when it happened. He was *there*! D'you see? He was *there*! "

The poor fellow was a Protestant and hence completely at sea in the intricacies of revealed religion. And I never can think of his experience without recalling something that happened years ago to me in Poland. I had travelled all the way from Warsaw to Cracow to interview a certain Prince of the Church. He was a great man, people said, robust and lively and genial, and sometimes outspoken with regard to the communist regime. I was hoping for some pungent comment on the struggle between Church and State; and naturally I had not undertaken this long and uncomfortable journey without first making sure that he was at home. What, then, was my chagrin when his chaplain declared, with much regret and many assurances of the delight which my visit would otherwise have caused, that his Eminence was away.

" But they told me he was here. Does he not wish to see the foreign press ? "

" Nothing, nothing of that sort ! It is just that he had to go away. *Il sera désolé !* " cried the chaplain, with passionate sincerity.

At this moment the Cardinal entered the vestibule and one by one his callers sank upon their knees and kissed his ring. I looked the chaplain full and steadily in the eye: he returned my gaze with perfect candour.

" Just for a minute or two," I pleaded.

" *Puisque je vous dis qu'il est absent !* "

" Is there any hope he might have a word with me, his absence notwithstanding ? "

" But how could he, Mademoiselle ? It is physically impossible," said the chaplain with a nip in his voice, and he turned away to bow respectfully as the Cardinal left the room.

It was a beautiful little example of the certitudes of Holy Church, a clear hint that the evidence of one's own two eyes, if conflicting with the pronouncements of higher authority, must be taken with a grain of salt. It was the failure of the Protestant editor to realize this that had led him into the scrape described; but he atoned for it by a willingness to learn. In due course he published an apology, agreeing that the event in question had, in fact, never taken place.

The pity of it is that people seldom or never stand up to an attack. The scales appear so hopelessly weighted against them that they collapse without firing a shot. I know only of one case in which a resistance was offered. An editor in

Dublin received a letter from a Bishop saying that one of his priests had asked leave to proceed against the paper and inviting him, before anything further happened, to offer an explanation. It is expected that a letter of this kind should be answered in a spirit of entire surrender, and with an almost tearful plea for lenience. The editor replied that the light rap on the knuckles administered to the obscure divine in question had been richly deserved, and gravely remarked that if it came to that, he was none too well pleased with the Bishop himself. Nothing more was heard of the matter.

I too have had my little brush with the clergy; and since it was conducted throughout on a level of sustained and extravagant lunacy that only Ireland can hope to reach, I will give some account of it. It was a long time ago. The scene was a little village where over a period of years I had often stayed, sometimes for months on end. The people there lived on the high imaginative plane where the small incidents of life become suffused with poetry and the large ones fall easily into their place. There was a peculiar excitement in being, a richness in the fabric of everyday life, that is rarely found in great cities. The capers of the gentry, the exploits of the poacher in chief, the startling procedures of a doctor, a robbery at the Big House and the attempts of the police to discover the author of it by divination, the cunning substitution of a goose at death's door for the hale goose that lived placidly in some one's barn, feuds, court cases, jokes, all provided the material for an unending local saga.

But for a year or two past the local discussions had tended to veer round to one particular matter. This was the building of a new parish house and the central figure of it was the parish priest. A delicious little rural comedy was in progress, of a kind which recurs again and again in the pattern of Irish country life: and, as I was then writing a series of Irish notes and sketches for a newspaper, it seemed to offer an appropriate subject. Not all of my friends in the village shared this view.

"Yerra, for God's sake! The old man will have your life!"

"Mind you, I said nothing!"

"Mind you, you hadn't it from me!"

"O Lord save us!"

The article appeared in the paper and broad smiles on many a face: there was a fearful glee in the air, a delicious tension, similar to that which follows the placing of a squib fairly and squarely in the headmaster's pocket. The Reverend Mother of the Convent dashed off a note to my hostess which was stinging but alas! without point, as the poor lady was in no way to blame. A pietist newspaper came out with a guarded editorial on the evils of anti-clericalism. And the parish priest brooded.

' Oh God, woman, been reading that article of yours: how long d'you think you'll be let stay in the country? " a friend had inquired, on my return to Dublin.

The affair had created a stir out of all relation to its importance. For one thing, priests are as much " news " in Ireland as are film stars in America: and for another, it is rarely that they are frankly criticized. The public tweaking of an ecclesiastical nose was the occasion of scandalized protest in some quarters, of rejoicing in others; and there was endless speculation as to whose nose it could be. Indeed, so many were the inquiries and suggestions on this point, so widely dotted about the map of Ireland were the parishes put forward as the probable scene that I had the impression most readers thought it was their own priest who had come under fire. For this reason it might have been wiser for the real hero to endure the restricted humiliation of his flock's amusement in dignified silence: but after three months of meditation he started proceedings for libel.

Weeks went by and nothing more was heard. Although I was joined in the action, no writ had come my way. I finished my assignment in Dublin and went on to another in Italy. During my absence a gnome appeared and endeavoured to serve the writ; and finding the bird had flown demanded at least to be given her address. My co-tenant in the house I then partly occupied was a man of great consideration and, as he put it in a letter to me, sensing that the call was not of a social nature he refused to yield up my address and offered instead to forward any correspondence on. It was subsequently reported in the newspapers that I had gone from Ireland leaving no address, but that a friend came round to my flat from time to time and collected my letters. About the same time a dear old lady I knew, the very soul of virtue and respectability, was suddenly and unaccountably visited by a uniformed policeman who badgered her for news of my whereabouts, glaring about him meanwhile as if he half-expected to find me under her sofa.

I returned to Ireland and sat patiently waiting for this writ to make its appearance. Month went past after month and nothing whatever was heard. And had it not been for the people in the remote little village that was the scene of the article, I should never have known what was happening until it burst upon me, in all its horror, in the newspapers. Well-informed and reliable as ever, they told a friend of mine of the full details of an impending settlement. Where did they get them? How did they know? It was another and a signal triumph of the local grapevine.

Thus within a few days of the hearing in Court I learned of the retractions and apologies the publishers had filed, not only in their name but, no doubt with the kindly intention of saving me trouble, in mine. There was no time to do more than to send a message to the plaintiff repudiating these documents and offering to fight it out alone. It must be

confessed that this was an unkind thing to do because the
legal actions of Irish clergy are brought on the assumption
that the defendants will play the game and surrender. But
the prospect of the Plaintiff's cross-examination entranced
me: the possibilities were too rich to forgo: I longed to
see how the rules of evidence would apply.

Legal representation was something of a problem. The
legal approach in Ireland differs from that in most western
countries at the best of times. Solicitors tend to look for a
cosy arrangement, like good uncles, rather than fight the
client's battle, and to find your man amicably working in
with the other side is no unfamiliar experience; and in the
actual Court proceedings, emotions and prejudices and racial
tics play a larger part than is customary elsewhere. The
prospects in a case of this kind were enough to make the
blood run cold.

"Don't get Catholic Counsel! he'll sell you down the
river," advised some experienced friends, themselves devout
Catholics: and others, "not a Protestant, for God's sake!
you'll have lost before you begin."

In despair I had toyed with the idea of engaging a Jew;
but there was a peril in this of Plaintiff's Counsel, by a
timely and delicate allusion to the Crucifixion, bringing my
whole case with a crash to the ground.

In the end Catholic Counsel was procured, a nice little man
who consented to act for me provided I allowed him to defend
rather than counter-attack. He did, and with immediate
effect. The priest received my challenge and, as soon as he
had recovered from the annoyance and shock, began to
retreat. He had no quarrel with me, it appeared: I had
merely written the article. Accordingly he would drop all
claims and proceedings against me and propose that my name
be struck from the records of the case.

There followed days of arguments between the legal

representatives of the three parties involved, while the hearing was adjourned time and again. The priest said I was not to be represented in Court: we replied that I should be. The priest then said that at least my Counsel was to do no more than confirm the arrangements he himself had proposed: we replied that we should make it clear that I was ready to defend the article. At this point the whole affair seemed to take a peculiar turn. There is so much in Ireland that every one knows but, for some occult reason, no one must say. The entire social fabric seems to quiver gently at the idea of even a small pale light being turned briefly on some of it. People curl up at the thought of exposure as a sea anemone curls at the touch of a stick. It was now quite clear to all that the Plaintiff in the case was on the run, and it became slowly but surely quite clear to me that there was a general desire to keep everything comfortably and decently covered up: and that this desire was shared to some extent, perhaps unconsciously, by my own solicitor.

That solicitor was a splendid fellow in every way. Joyously he took up a case from which many Dublin lawyers would have recoiled in horror. He fought like a lion. He took unheard-of liberties with the facts. Leaving me more dead than alive with fright, for example, he would go off and cheerfully assure the enemy that his client was fighting mad and fit to be tied up and that nothing less than total, bloody, decisive battle would content her. My character, in his hands, became something to frighten the crows. Stress was laid on my complete irresponsibility, the time I had spent in patiently mugging up Church scandals of every description, the eagerness with which I sought an opportunity of ventilating them. The possibility of an impassioned speech in Court was not to be entirely ruled out. I had seen myself as a crusader in the cause of truth and justice: my solicitor rubbed tirelessly in the fact that I was a dangerous lunatic.

The enemy now was retiring with more haste than dignity. The moment seemed ripe to press home the attack, to pursue him, to harry his rear and pinch his flank until the whole thing fizzled on a note of Dublin farce. But at this point all initiative seemed to pass from me in a most mysterious way; I had a sense of being still in the best and kindest of hands, but without any particular say in my own affairs. It may have been the concern of my lawyer for a client apparently resolved on suicide; and it may have been that all the while he was so brilliantly conducting our campaign the black waters of the bog were striving atavistically in his mind with the pure fountains of Trinity College. All that is sure is that one moment I was being advised to accept an arrangement which partly saved the priest's face as well as my own: at the next I was being warmly praised for my common sense in so doing. To this day I cannot recall having done anything of the kind. And the insults I hurl at my friend the solicitor whenever we meet evoke nothing but bursts of delighted chuckles.

There remained, then, only the pleasures of a spectator. The tribe had taken over and was managing things in its own immensely capable way to suit itself. At last we all assembled in Court once more. Two faces were absent this time: those of the Plaintiff and his solicitor, who had withdrawn to the country in a state of only partial satisfaction.

After the arrangement concerning myself had been dealt with Counsel for the Plaintiff got down to business. Deeply regretting the unpleasant necessity, he read out the offending article from beginning to end. No doubt it was really considered necessary. There was a feel in the air of that Court, a *nuance*, which gave one rather to think but which was too slight, too indefinable, to justify allegations to the contrary. But whether he did or did not feel obliged to repeat it, the result was to give the newspapers a chance to reprint the story in full and with impunity, causing further glee among those subversive elements who had happened to miss the earlier publication. One almost felt a touch of sympathy for the priest. His idea no doubt, had been to assert himself before the parish and to demonstrate once again, as if further demonstration were needed, what happened to those who spoke out of turn in Ireland. Nothing surely could have been further from his mind than to have the whole episode churned up again.

Next Counsel read out the true story of the priest and the parish house. It was a simple statement, unsworn and not accompanied by any evidence: and, since it referred to the Plaintiff in flattering terms, could hardly have been prepared by himself. Not a single point in my article was allowed to be true except my description of the roof as red. Not one of the things I believed I had seen nor of those I thought I had heard but was the figment of my clearly diseased imagination. I thought of the Cardinal in Cracow.

The apology of the publishers was read out, and the offer made of a large sum to a Catholic charity. The Judge wound up the case and expressed appreciation of the fact that the reverend gentlemen would leave the Court as poor a man as he entered it. He may well have been unaware that the reverend gentleman's initial claim had mentioned the sum of five thousand pounds as appropriate damages. No doubt no word was spoken by any one in the Court that day but was pure and honest and devoid of malicious ambiguity. But when all was over the barristers and solicitors engaged in the case assembled in the hall outside and giggled as learned and distinguished legal gentlemen can seldom have giggled before.

IX

A FEROCIOUS ANTI-CLERICAL

"LE soif des Irlandais pour la liberté," said a distinguished French writer once, "est connu dans
le monde entier." He was addressing a Dublin
audience and beautifully saying the right things one after
the other in a honeyed stream. Here and there in the hall
a keen observer might perhaps have noticed a jaw suddenly
drop, a pair of eyes grow dull and glassy, but for the most
part the listeners leaned back and glowed with satisfaction.
A celebrated man had come all the way from Paris to recite
the national creed to them in a foreign tongue and although
there might be chuckles and waggings of the head later on
for the moment they were giving themselves up to the
pleasure of it.

The creed says plainly that the longing for freedom is
one of the deepest the Irish know: that the long martyrdom
of their history arose out of a refusal to accept the yoke, and
that for liberty's dear sake they were and are always ready
to sacrifice themselves and their all. The trouble about this
creed, as about most others, is that it is so hard to believe it
true. We are invited to agree that here is a race of heroes
and we are hard put to it to remember meeting any one who
appeared even normally sturdy. I believe I could name a
dozen Irishmen, perhaps, who if goaded sufficiently far might
be capable of saying Boo ! to a goose; and half of them, I
suspect, would treat the goose simultaneously to a furtive and
reassuring wink. " Don't mind me," that deft, conspiratorial
closing of an eye would say: " I'm only codding ! "

Shortly after the events described in the previous chapter,

I was back in Dublin in the company of friends. They began to discuss a man down in the centre of the country somewhere, speaking of him in awed tones as a ferocious anti-clerical. I cocked an ear to it for I had never met any such person in Ireland. The country seethes with anti-clericalism, as is only natural, but you do not meet avowed, self-styled and as it were practising anti-clericals. Of all labels this is a most unfortunate one to acquire and one most carefully avoided by men of ordinary prudence. For one thing, it is extremely bad for business.

" Oh, he's a terror, that fellow. Oh, he's desperate," some one said, with deep admiration.

" What he's been through ! "

" A martyr, you might say."

" Go and see him. Don't miss him. Oh, he'll tell you things . . ."

I carefully noted down his name—they didn't know the address—resolving to visit him at the earliest opportunity. The others too joined in urging me to lose no time: from the way they spoke one gathered that at any moment his activities might land him in gaol or at least on the England boat.

" He knows who you are. He knows all about you."

" He'll give you the real low-down."

" Tell him we sent you."

I returned home pleased and happy at the thought of this new contact. Ireland is a country to arouse affection rather than esteem and the rare little flashes of spirit are precious as flowers in winter. Yet as long as there were men like this unknown ready to defy impossible odds, to suffer for their integrity, perhaps—who knows ?—to go down in a defeat more glorious than victory could ever be . . .

This train of thought was interrupted by the telephone.

" Is that you ? " said a guarded voice. " I've been

thinking over what . . . what was said. Are you really going to see X ? " [1]

Indeed I was.

" Well, do you think you'll be writing about him at all ? "

That was my expectation. A pause followed. When the voice spoke again it had dropped to a still lower key.

" You'll be reticent, I suppose ? You'll not refer to the matter we touched on ? "

This was a little disconcerting. Here at last, it seemed, was an Irishman sailing fearlessly under his own true colours: and I did not see how adequately to celebrate his courage without some mention of it creeping into the story.

" But why on earth not ? "

" Because," the voice said, with just a suspicion of hoarseness, " there'd be trouble. There'd be no end of trouble."

J reflected on this.

" How would it be if I promised to show you the manuscript first ? "

" That's the great girl ! " sang the voice, delightedly. " You're a great old girl all the same. I told them you were all right ! "

I sat there for some time turning this conversation over in my mind in growing excitement. I knew numbers of militant anti-clericals in France and Italy but not one of them ever had shunned publicity. In fact they spared no pains to draw the world's attention to their views on every occasion that offered. What, then, could be the fearful activities of this young Irishman, on what desperate work was he engaged, that a misplaced word could bring it all to nothing ? Was he perhaps the king-pin of a secret resistance movement ? No other explanation seemed possible. I seized a pen and wrote a few lines saying I should be in the neigh-

[1] Readers will understand that he cannot be named.

bourhood shortly to view the *famous ruins* and hoped to make his acquaintance then. Surely the name and the town would be sufficient address ? I laughed to think of the local post-master steaming open the envelope and puzzling over my carefully non-committal phrases.

X never replied to my letter and, after waiting some days I packed up things for a night or two and set out to beard him in his lair. The journey was accomplished under conditions of pleasant normality. Rain fell heavily from start to finish: the train went more slowly than one would have thought possible: there was an hour's wait for the bus at the other end. The town itself consisted of one street about two miles long with whiskery lanes sprouting from it on either side: a stone monument to a hero of the Irish Resistance: a large new Catholic Church and a large old and decrepit Protestant Church: a pile of ruins heaped on a meadow near by: and any number of bars. I went into the best, and indeed the only, hotel and having engaged a room inquired of the Boots in a confidential mutter if he knew a Mr. X.

" Mr. X, is it ? " said the Boots in clear loud tones. " Mr. X lodges with Miss Y."

I looked hastily round to see if any one was within earshot and went on: " Is Miss Y on the telephone ? "

" She is not," said the Boots. " And you wouldn't find him there if she was. He's up at the ——[1] all day."

" What does he do at the —— ? " I inquired softly.

" He's in charge of it," said the Boots. " Isn't it shocking weather we have ? You've lost your voice, I see. There's a fire in the parlour if you want to dry out."

I went into the parlour to dry out and, at the further suggestion of the Boots, took a drop of what wouldn't poison me while he leaned comfortably against the mantelpiece and engaged in conversation.

[1] Readers will understand that X's occupation cannot be revealed.

" If you want to see Mr. X," he began, " the finest thing you can do is to sit there until he comes. He'll be in on his way home to lunch—in and out—it wouldn't do to be late."

Here the Boots was overcome with merriment at thoughts of his own.

" If by any chance you miss him now," he presently resumed, " he'll be in again at half-five. In and out once more: he has his tea at six." The Boots broke down again at this, then pulled himself together and went on: " In the ordinary way he'd be back at seven and stay till closing time with the schoolmaster and the chemist. But I doubt if you'll see him to-night at all. The Redemptorists are here."

The Redemptorists ! What had they to do with it ?

" He'd be at the Mission, d'ye see ? " said the Boots, noticing my astonishment.

" But does Mr. X go in for Missions ? "

" It isn't the question of going in or of not going in," explained the Boots. " It's the question of being seen anywhere else while they're on."

So ! The man's duplicity took my breath away. I determined next to sound this Boots and find out how far he was in the secret.

" What sort of person is Mr. X ? "

" A decent poor man," he replied. " Very nervous: oh, highly nervous," he added, smiling broadly.

" An speaks Irish," he went on, as one might say: understands nuclear fission. " He's after translating The Canterbury Tales into the Irish. Oh, he's the finest scholar in the country."

" And what does he think of . . . of things ? "

" What things ? " inquired the Boots, staring.

" Of . . . things in general," I said with a *fin sourire*.

The Boots considered me thoughtfully. Honesty was

written all over his large pink face and in another moment, I am persuaded, he would have told me all. But the door suddenly opened and a female voice wailed: "Willy! the bags for No. 18!" and the spell was broken. He set off at a rapid pace for the door.

"Ah, we couldn't expect he'd tell us that," he said, and vanished.

I moved into the public bar and sat waiting for the redoubtable, if two-faced, X to arrive. It was full of men in tweed coats discussing their business affairs in undertones which sank from time to time to a whisper. A woman sidled up to the counter and purchased a bottle of port which she carefully wrapped in brown paper and concealed in her shopping basket. Then came a little company of three, of which two members were indulgently supporting the third. A burly farmer with the cheeks of a mandrill came next: then in trotted a little fellow with a pale moon face and wisps of fair hair tumbling over a high forehead: and then at last a man whom I felt instinctively could be none other than X himself. He was tall and thin and dressed in black, with an aquiline nose and deepset eyes in which there smouldered a sombre, fanatical light: his whole bearing spoke of a ruthless determination.

The barman moved from behind the bar and came over to my table. "Was it you the lady looking for Mr. X? He's just come in. Will I tell him?"

The news that a stranger had arrived and was inquiring for one of the citizens had of course gone round the hotel like a streak of lightning. I thanked the barman and asked him to be so kind; and, to my surprise, he went across and muttered something in the ear not of the tall man in black but of the little moon-faced person who started violently and threw an imploring glance round the room before shambling reluctantly in my direction.

" Are you Mr. X ? " I cried. " I had somehow got it into my head it was that man over there."

" Oh God, that's Tommy Lynch the egg-tester," mumbled Mr. X. " I can't stop now . . . wish I'd known you were coming . . . had no idea."

" But I wrote to you last week."

" And I got the letter ! " he said, with a faint glimmer of triumph. " Oh, I got the letter all right. Where is it ? "

He fished in his pocket and drew a crumpled envelope which he held up as if refuting by material evidence a statement to the contrary.

" But I thought it was those fellows in Dublin pulling my leg," he explained, carefully putting the letter away again. " They're terrible jokers. You don't want to mind them. What's the time ? Sacred Heart ! She'll eat me ! I must be off. Listen. I'll send a message to the works to say I'm ill and I'll meet you here at half-two and show you the town. Good-bye now."

He was out of the bar as fast as his little legs could carry him, leaving me open-mouthed in wonder. I seemed to have arrived plumb in the middle of a crisis in the affairs of this poor hunted man. All the stories I had ever heard of the misfortune lying in wait for Irish anti-clericals rose up in my mind and I began considering ways in which it might be possible to help him. The friendly barman paused again in the act of collecting glasses.

" He didn't stay long with you, then," he remarked.

" He seemed to have the divil behind him ! "

" It's his landlady, d'you see," the barman revealed. " She's great on punctuality. Oh, he's in dread of her."

In one of the books of Somerville and Ross there is a passage describing how an earnest English scholar went out to hear pure Irish songs by native singers and was treated to a vulgar ditty in English about—as far as my memory goes—

somebody's cow; and how he coldly laid down his pen like a reporter during an unimportant speech. I mentally laid down my pen and closed my notebook At the same time that dizziness, that vertigo, so recurring a sensation in Ireland and to which I have alluded elsewhere, came on with an ugly rush. The phrase of a French novelist about certain young revolutionaries in France: *Ils veulent réorganiser l'univers et ils tremblent devant le concierge!* flashed across my mind. There was a strong inclination to write X off and to return at once to Dublin, where a complaint would be lodged with his friends.

But then came the sense of a possible injustice. In the first place I knew nothing of Miss Y, the landlady in question. It might be that she was in fact more formidable than the Hierarchy and the Knights of Columbanus and Maria Duce all massed together: Irish landladies of this description are not unknown. Or perhaps she was not formidable at all and it was simply that poor X was more than usually subject to the terror, the moral paralysis, that afflicts so many Irishmen in their dealings with the female sex. Or perhaps every drop of his courage and resolution went into his great fight, leaving none to spare for the trifling events of everyday life, so that he was in the position of those heroes who cover themselves with glory in the field but on the domestic front are the veriest cravens. Or perhaps, again—and this seemed likeliest of all—Miss Y had the only lodgings in town so tha anything but the most unqualified submission might leave him without a roof over his head.

The character of X began to assume a pleasing ambiguity. Punctually at half past two he appeared, rather calmer and more at his ease, carrying a case full of books. These, he explained, were the collected works of the poet Longfellow which he would lend to me if I promised to send them back again: he had written his name in each. My thanks he waved gracefully aside.

" It's little enough I can do for you," he said. " It's not very often we get literary ladies down here."

We set out for a tour of the town. I had already taken in the salient features from the corner of my eye as we rode through it that morning in the bus, but now was able to observe it in greater detail. Outside the butcher's shop, exposed to the weather, hung a row of joints of the most extraordinary shapes and sizes, as if the butcher had suddenly gone berserk and snatching up a chopper had laid about him in all directions. A yellow dog lay peacefully asleep in the middle of the road, with the traffic mounting the pavement each side in order not to disturb his rest. On the church gate a hand-painted notice with two spelling mistakes announced that owing to the welcome presence of the Redemptorist Fathers in the town there would be no dance on Sunday. At each street-corner stood little groups of motionless men with their collars turned up, hoping perhaps for a bicycle accident or something else to discuss.

" A beautifully peaceful existence," I remarked.

X gave a little moan.

He proved himself a tireless guide and a fascinating companion, having the whole inside story of the town's affairs at his finger-ends and being perfectly willing to share it. A native of County Mayo, he regarded the rest of Ireland with suspicion and this small patch of it in particular as a blot on the world's face. He spent some time trying to persuade me that the local people were the meanest and most rapacious as well as the most ill-natured and evil-spoken in the whole of the country; and poured out his words with such despairing conviction that, if I had not heard similar claims made for every little Irish town I had ever known, he might almost have won me over. But while he made sardonically merry at the expense of the local political bosses, describing their ventures and mishaps in the fields of commerce, sport and love with a kind of dismal relish, on the clerical question he was utterly silent. It was noticeable, further, that whenever we passed a man in priestly garb he swept off his hat with the same faintly priggish zeal as anyone else and once, when a Dominican asked him the way, went so far as to throw down a newly lighted cigarette before he answered.

There was no use in waiting for him to reveal himself or attempting slowly to draw him out. I determined to try the frontal attack which often succeeds with Irishmen because they are so used to oriental deviations and circumlocutions that the surprise of it catches them off their guard. There was a colleague of mine once in a Dublin office from whom towards the end of the month I would sometimes borrow money and who was always immensely diverted by the bold, unprefaced requests I made, unlike those of my other, subtler colleagues who would delicately and methodically work round to the point, leaving it even then so vague as to entail no loss of face if a blank were drawn. He seemed to regard this candour as a funny English habit out of which I should presently grow; and yet the result of it invariably was that his hand flew into his trouser pocket and out again with the specified number of coins before his normal defences were even alerted.

Bearing this in mind, I waited a suitable moment. Presently three nuns came out of a house and glided along the pavement in front of us like three black coffins walking on end.

" It is said," I remarked, casually, " that a law from the bad old times, entitling one to shoot at sight any priest, friar or nun wearing religious habits on the highroad, has never actually been repealed."

My companion turned his head towards me hesitantly, as if doubtful at first of having heard aright, and all at once his round pale face was suffused with joy. His wide dreamy blue eyes positively sparkled. For a moment or two he savoured the proposition in silence: and then he said reflectively, " It might, however, be well to check that before . . ."

" Oh, mind you I wasn't proposing . . ."

" Of course not."

And presently as we left the mean little streets and walked under dripping trees towards the ruin he unburdened his soul. It was a strangely complicated story, made still more difficult to follow by the excessive caution with which it was told. Anything in the nature of a clear question he parried with amazing deftness. In his student days he had either written or said something, but he declined to reveal what. Someone had naturally written an anonymous letter to a Bishop: " The Island of Saints and Informers," he quoted, smiling resignedly. Then there had begun a chain of persecutions, although here again he did not disclose the forms they had taken. Police bobbed vaguely up in the narrative only to disappear without their precise rôle in it ever coming to light. The shadow of another landlady fell across the picture and darkened it further, one knew not how. The mother and sisters of X had, in some curious manner, been put to public shame. Another unexplained result of it all was that X could never go to Galway again as long as he lived. And it was thanks to this episode and all that grew out of it that he was sleepless, wanting in ambition, inclined to stammer and afraid of his shadow.

But what had happened ?

" The boys in Dublin may have told you I am an anti-clerical," he remarked gravely. " Do you wonder at it ? "

No, no, indeed I did not. In any case my capacity for wonder was exhausted. We stood in silence looking at the ruin, with the words UP DEV smeared along one side in tar, and the sopping bits of paper strewn about the ground and the orange peels and the broken bottles and the weeping sky.

" And what are you doing ? " I inquired at last.

" In my free time I am reading the masterpieces of world literature one by one."

No, I meant, about . . .

" Oh, that. Nothing," said X, simply and sublimely.

Nothing ?

" Nothing at all. You see," he explained, " I can't. There would be trouble. No end of it. And, by the way, please don't pass on to any one else the story I have just told you. Just keep it under your hat."

X

EVENING IN CORK

IRELAND glows to the inward eye in all the colours of
the rainbow; it is one of her many little tricks. Home
the exiles come with the fire of longing, stoked by
evenings of reminiscence in the company of admiring
foreigners, fanned by the breeze of their own imaginative
powers, burning merrily in their hearts—and what does the
jade do but clothe herself before their adoring eyes in the dull
even grey of a prison uniform. Impishly she continues in this
sober apparel until, maddened, they arrange to depart: then,
when the tickets are bought and the trunks labelled, she
appears for a moment again in her finery.

Hence the determination of any one who has spent some
time in Dublin, capital of poetry, charm, wit *et tout ça*, is to
get out of it whatever the cost and inconvenience. Galway,
Sligo, even Limerick assume in his fancy the most inviting
shapes. He chases from one to the other and even as he
arrives they dissolve into nothing. He rattles around the
country like a shrivelled nut in a roomy shell. Presently he
begins to feel that after all Dublin is not so bad: he hastens
eagerly back, to find that it is worse.

A prey to the fidgets, I decided to pay a visit to Cork. A
vision of her colour-washed quays, her ornate façades, her
unexpected little squares and waterways rose up and
beckoned. Shandon bells pealing out, the sing-song voices,
the rough country-people leading their carts through the
main streets as if in a village, the gossip and intrigue, ships
hooting down the river: surely here was life, colour,
movement?

Alas! the only truly impressive thing in Cork I remembered, as the train rolled in, is its lunatic asylum. It is remarkable even for Ireland, a sparsely populated land where only the pious and the unhinged assemble in any number. Contemplating it, the stranger may be overwhelmed by a sudden delicious panic: he may feel sure he is entering a city of passion, of violence, frantic with ambition and tormented by doubt, distracted by love and hate to a point where all but the strongest minds are overthrown. But if so he will be disappointed, for Cork does not live up to its asylum at all: it is a snoring, muffled little place, dazzled by nothing but the prospect of its own excellence.

The true satisfaction felt by the people of Cork when they consider their town and themselves, their evident belief that, safely arrived in Cork, it is unnecessary to look further, are the pleasantest things imaginable. The first time I encountered the Cork spirit was in Paris, and I remember yet the glow of admiration it awoke in me. I was assured that the ladies of Cork were not only the handsomest in Ireland but among the most elegant in Europe: and that those Parisiennes who wished to be really *chic* were in the habit of sending to Cork for their clothes. The speaker, who came from Cork, was a nice young woman dressed, as I recall, in a tweed skirt and a mauve knitted jersey. She had been educated in England and resident in Paris for several years, and we could not have blamed her if, among all these alien influences, her vision of the splendours of home had rather faded. There was a magnificence in the conception which appealed to me strongly then and still more so when, some time later, I went to Cork and found that it was unsupported by visual evidence. Pride in a manifest excellence is natural and human and yet there is something dull about it, a touch of the prosaic, compared with this other pride that is rooted in faith and nourished by fancy.

I came to Cork in the late afternoon, as the rain was finishing for the day and the shop girls were all hurrying home in their smart coats of emerald, saffron or puce. The landlady brought me my tea of cold ham and raw tomatoes and plum cake and invited me to her evening recitation of the rosary: an opportunity, she said, which none of her ladies or gentlemen ever willingly missed. And so I invented an engagement and fled from the lace curtains and the Infant of Prague and the smell of old, boiled cabbage into the streets again, with nothing to do until bed-time. All that Cork was offering that night in the way of distraction was the life of Blessed Martin de Porres at the Metropolitan Opera House, by permission of the Dominican Fathers: three or four American films, full of lust, crime and violence; and an illustrated talk on the Sacred Shroud. The fading sunlight fell sweetly on the river while the burghers sat at home and brooded over the rise in the cost of living.

I decided to go in search of my friend the Professor. Although I had no address for him I was sure that a man of his eminence and habits could be tracked down. The last time we were in company he had been magnificently holding court in Clancy's bar, and thither I turned my steps: but it was empty this evening save for a party of workmen flirting with a local Cleopatra who had but a single tooth in her head—and that one plumb in the middle of the upper jaw —which she constantly bared with delight at their sallies. From time to time she treated me, in feminine solidarity, to a wink and I winked back, marvelling a little at the sweet power of sex that could make light of so grave a disadvantage: and then reluctantly, as the fun grew faster and more furious, and the jokes racier, went on my way.

I crossed the river and climbed up to Sunday's Well, where the Professor was rumoured to have his lodging. The sun had set by now, leaving the sky vermilion, and a pearly mist was creeping steadily up from the water and engulfing the trees beside it. The steep crooked lanes, with the black-shawled figures ascending and descending noiseless in the twilight, had a romantic, Spanish air. In Rider's Inn the people shook their heads.

"The Professor didn't come in for ages. We were wondering was he ill."

A series of calls to similar establishments produced identical results. It began to look as if he had renounced conviviality, which would have been sad enough, or removed to some other place, which would have been bitter. There would be a gap in the life of Cork if there were no longer the possibility that round the corner at any time might heave that vast jovial figure, puffing a little with the strain of motion, pausing occasionally to mop its trickling brow as with purposeful bearing it moved towards the parlour of its choice. I ran up to passers-by in the street and laid my problem before them. All showed a kindly interest, many gave excellent advice. Gathering in a little knot, they pooled their scraps of information and their experience for my benefit and we narrowed the likely places of lodging to three. A maid in one of them said the Professor lived there but was out.

" At this time of night he's apt to be in Tony's above, but I will just verify that," she said and withdrew, reappearing in a moment to say: " My surmise was correct."

At Tony's above they revealed that, since it was Wednesday, the Professor would be at O'Mahoney's below, but they expected him back a little later on in the evening. And at Mahoney's below he was, surrounded by friends and admirers, rosy and warm, snorting with glee over an idea which had just struck him, with his spectacles slipping awry on his short nose.

One of the strange and endearing things about Ireland is

a perpetual work of reconciliation with herself that she carries on. She offends, she disgusts, she wounds, she can nauseate, and then suddenly and as it were absentmindedly she displays another side of herself as on a dark night the clouds will sometimes break apart and briefly reveal a star: and the sufferer realizes, not without weariness, not indeed without gloomy foreboding, that there cannot be an end just yet. At times I have been reduced by the pressure of malice, of treachery practised less for the sake of gaining a victory than from a gnomish delight in treachery itself, to a state of mind where I would hesitate to open the front door or answer the telephone. I have slunk about the streets of Dublin squinting this way and that in dread of meeting a familiar eye, in the timid, furtive way of one who owes large sums of money or believes the secret police to be on his trail. Then just as things are at their worst somebody will do or say a thing so magnificent, and which could hardly be done or said in any other place, that once again, for the time being, the quarrel is patched up. And in the same way Ireland redeems herself by a small number of her people, for whose sake she must be forgiven a great deal. Of these the Professor is one.

He had just been explaining with a nice blend of lucidity and fantasy his theory of the Inferiority Simplex, which he illustrated by means of a diagram with mathematical symbols, to three or four of his Boswells and, as I came in, called in a rich carrying voice for a round of drinks. He seemed to regard my unearthing of him as a brilliant stroke of police work and wished to hear every move in it, now nodding approval, now shaking his head as I mentioned some place whose doors he would darken no more. A more easy-going and sunny-minded man it would have been hard to find, but once a publican had refused him drink after hours it was the end: he would show no mercy.

It was perhaps for this reason that he cherished a

tenderness for Galway, where such a thing happens but
rarely. Once I had come on him there smiling to himself
among the grey stones and splashing waters and he had burst
forth in the praise of the city, saying there was a feel of
timelessness, of eternity, in the air. They *never* close ! he cried.
I had come with the intention of collecting material for an
article but was swept into the Professor's train instead: we
spent the rest of the day agreeably and profitably in a little
bar off the market square, with the rain pattering down outside, my friend dominating the scene inside, effortlessly
entertaining the assembly for hour after hour and disposing
of stray hecklers with the lightning strokes of irrelevance of
which he was a master.

" You third-rate music-hall mesmerist ! " he would roar,
out of the blue, at some little man who had opposed him too
confidently.

This evening he was a little inclined to be querulous
about a recent book by Frank O'Connor, in which Cork was
described as a hell-hole. The Professor was free from the
normal touchiness of Corkmen on the subject of Cork, as he
was from all vulgar prejudice, but he felt that the expression
was rather too strong. A hole Cork might possibly be, but
" hell-hole " showed a lack of restraint on the writer's part
and further made the place out more exciting than it was.

" The man's no drinker, of course," he remarked, as if
extravagance of every kind were to be expected in the
circumstances; but I told him how once I had met Frank
O'Connor at tea-time and stayed drinking with him in the
Pearl Bar until after nine, and as he listened he nodded
approvingly, his features relaxed and slowly resumed their
cherubic benevolence. He was not the man to do another
an injustice.

We continued at O'Mahoney's below for a space.
Presently he announced his intention of taking me to dinner

in the city, and the party broke up. He looked a little gloomily after the retreating figure of one of his young friends.

"I'm afraid his mother disapproves of me," he said. "She says I encourage him to drink. The truth is, of course, I'm trying to save him from it."

We took a bus and bowled away down to Patrick Street, getting down at the statue of Father Mathew, the famous advocate of temperance. He was a good man and fought a great fight, but he never explained how life in Ireland was to be lived once the drink was put down; and now he stood on his pedestal, solitary and respected, with the consumption rising yearly round him.

It was perhaps the sight of that motionless figure which put it into the Professor's mind that half past eight was after all very early to dine and we might just as well wet our whistle at Clancy's first: and thither we turned our steps. To accompany him anywhere was like taking part in a Roman triumph, such was the majesty of his gait and the warmth of popular acclaim: everyone knew him, hats were raised and the Boots of the Victoria Hotel sang out "You're in good hands, ma'am, I see." At Clancy's there was a cry of "You found him so!" from the charmer with the single tooth who was still enthroned and, seeing me in masculine company, dealt another prodigious wink.

The evening began to assume a familiar shape and to follow a well-worn pattern. There was an easing of intellectual fibre, a willingness to concede that Cork after all was the hub of the universe. The very idea of dinner was dismissed with contempt. Warm new friendships sprang up, and embittered arguments were conducted with total strangers: the Professor told long funny stories in Irish. From time to time one or another would think of a little place that really deserved a visit and out we streeled on to the pavement again. And all the time the clocks were ticking and their hands were moving on to that point where the inexorable " Now, sirs, please ! ", cruellest words in the English language, would be heard all over the city.

To-night we had a most unusual and unpleasant experience. As the final port of call we had resolved on a delightful place lying a little way out of the town. It was barely five minutes after closing-time when we arrived, our thirst for light and warmth and merriment still unassuaged, but to our grief they refused to open up: we battered against the door in vain. From inside came the sounds of revelry and good cheer, peals of laughter, the tinkle of an aged piano: it was more than flesh and blood could endure.

" Travellers ! " I bawled. " Bona fide travellers ! "

The door then opened an inch, allowing those within to catch a glimpse of the Professor's well-known form silhouetted against the lamplight, and shut again with a decided bang. A car drove up and two men got out.

" Travellers from Kenmare ! " they mumbled into the keyhole.

The door opened to admit them, as swiftly as if Kenmare had been a magic word. We tried to pass inside in their wake but the door was slammed again to our noses

" Bona fide travellers from Bandon ! " we howled. " You've let in the Kenmare men and now you shut the door on bona fides from Bandon ! "

There was real moral indignation in our voices, a genuine note of grievance, but no answering sound came from within, save that of the chain being dragged into place across the door. The Professor was as nearly downcast as it was possible for him to be.

" I hate this captious spirit ! " he groaned.

It was not the injustice of the thing we felt as much as the surly, un-Irish way in which it was done. As we made the return journey to Sunday's Well, the Professor's bearing was that of Napoleon gazing upon the fires of Moscow, or of some great spirit overthrown by blind unreasoning powers beyond its control. From time to time his noble head wove gently from side to side, like that of a fretting elephant. He drew, more than once, my attention to the way in which law-abiding English behaviour was insidiously creeping back into a land which had rejected it, ostensibly, for ever. Further, he pointed out that since he was the publican's mascot and no public house was ever raided with himself inside it the fools might shortly expect to be hoist with their own petard.

But as we passed through the darkness of one of the lanes that led to his house, a thought came to him and he rapped gently with his knuckles on a lighted window. The light went out as if he had shot it but the door opened and there was a hoarse whisper of " Come on in, Professor ! The boys is here." We went into a tiny snug the size of a horse-box with a wooden bench running round the wooden walls on which some dozen men were tightly squeezed together. At the sight of us, they squeezed up closer still so that we too could fit in and we stayed for an hour in those horrid surroundings, intensely uncomfortable, hardly able to draw a breath without cracking a neighbour's rib, afraid to speak for fear of the enemies in the street, and gave ourselves up to the pure, unalloyed, native pleasure of illegal drinking. It was beautiful to see the Professor flow and expand once more.

I have introduced him as a remarkable man, and so he is; but readers will no doubt have expected to find some of his quips and maxims reproduced here, in support of that claim and for them to savour and ponder at their leisure. It is clearly up to me to provide this evidence, or I shall be like those novelists who assert that one of their characters is a genius without depicting him subsequently in such a way as to make it appear likely. But the Professor is not only a mighty intelligence and the *raison d'être* for Cork city. He is also, as may have emerged, a convinced and valiant drinker and it is all I can do to keep up with him, cup for cup, without committing to memory the pearls of wisdom and wit that roll from his lips in a perpetual and effortless stream. When in his company I am brilliantly entertained, but I cannot afterwards remember how. There have been gala sessions indeed, after which I have woken without the faintest recollection of what the subject under discussion had been at all, and only the dimmest idea of where we had been and of how I had ever got home.

XI

ON TO BANDON

BANDON is an hour's ride on a bus from Cork and the official guide book does not make it out as an interesting place. It lists the various churches and banks, gives the population as 2,839, describes it as a large town in the centre of a rich agricultural district, remarks that Early Closing is on Thursday and with a fragment of history concludes. Passing idly through, you might see in it just another dead-alive little Irish town, with ugly shops and pretty houses, a river, a brewery, ruins here and there, church bells incontinently chiming and a deadly boredom always creeping in and always staved off with drink and prayers and scandal and bridge.

What makes Bandon interesting is that it has a Protestant community of over a thousand, more than one in three of its whole population. Once upon a time it was a Protestant colony where Catholics were not allowed entry at all. It is said that a single exception was made for a Catholic cobbler, since no Protestant cobbler was to be found, on condition that he went to church every Sunday: and that the poor fellow used nearly to kill himself running three miles beyond the walls of the town to Mass and back again in time for the morning service. One hopes that the story is true. There is a kind of redeeming sanity in the Protestants' recognition that, Scarlet Woman or no Scarlet Woman, shoes must be mended; and in the cobbler's view that, sin or no sin, he must provide for his family; although of course we may be flattering him here, for the decrees of the eternal and immutable Church vary from time to time and place to place

and it may in those days have been no sin, merely an extravagance, to run all that way to a house of Protestant worship.

Such exclusiveness is repugnant to the minds of men
to-day, having become impracticable; but the town still
offers a fascinating picture of religious differences in Ireland.
It is refreshing also to find the Protestants strong enough to
be able, as it were, to answer back. The pity is that they are
divided into five groups, Church of Ireland, Methodists,
Baptists, Plymouth Brethren and Cooneyites, or Dippers.
It is not therefore as a united body that they can front the
claims, and thwart the manœuvres, of Mother Church:
nevertheless they can give better account of themselves than
is elsewhere possible. In consequence religious—or party—
feeling runs high, with the Knights of Columbanus unusually
active for even so active a body, and the Protestants holding
together with the indomitable spirit of an army beleaguered,
yet with provisions for many months to come.

A moving example of their solidarity took place on the
very day of my visit. Two Colonels of the old school live in
the neighbourhood and both are fond of giving an occasional
lecture on the various parts of the British Empire in which
they had formerly seen service. According to report, one of
them was lively and entertaining and the other prosy; but the
second was either unaware of this estimation or else disagreed
with it, and the first had only to give a talk on the Punjab, for
example, for him to counter immediately with another on
Burma. It was Burma that evening; and although the Protestants had a very modest expectation of the treat before them
since, apart from anything else, they had in fact heard this particular lecture the year before, they turned out manfully to pay
their shilling and fill the hall. They would not have it said that
one of their number had lectured to empty space: they were
ready, in the spirit of their ancestors, to suffer for their beliefs.

As evening falls they gather in their homes and sing hymns

while the Catholics, no less sturdily, recite the rosary. It is impressive to find people caring deeply about such things as religious dogma in the world of to-day. Coming into this doctrinaire little society from the easy, secular atmosphere of Europe one may be tempted to chuckle; but before yielding to the temptation one should pause and consider if a chuckle here might not be similar to the insane and vulgar mirth of a yokel confronted by something new in his experience. For clearly, if these things ever mattered at all, they matter as much now as they did four hundred years ago. Few people to-day, even in Ireland, would worry their heads as to how many angels could dance on the point of a pin; and, while most will see in this a proof of increasing wisdom, it may equally well be a sign of decadence. The shelving of this matter of angels and pins may reveal no more than a lamentable falling-off. If, on the other hand, it and similar definitions of heavenly matters are in fact without substance or reality, they were so then as they are now. We should have, in that case, to admit that in the history of the world there had been a considerable waste of time.

Bandon, therefore, is either sublime or ridiculous: it is not a question on which the author of this book can have an opinion, but it does seem worthy of a mention in the official guide.

Religion in Ireland is an absorbing theme altogether. There is no religious indifference, no large body of people vaguely agnostic and yet vaguely following the Christian ethic, as in England. Every Gentile is either Catholic or Protestant, and nearly all of them go to Church every Sunday. Moreover, it is important, to know to which body the person you are speaking to belongs. The Irish are fond of making merry over the English habit of putting a stranger into his social category and over the irritation they feel when unable to " place " him; but nothing could be more comical than their own anxiety to find out whether he is " Prod " or " Cat " and the lengths to which they go, the elaborate strategy, the subtle devices, they use in order to do so. No holds are barred save the question direct. What is more, there is as much snobbery of a social kind in their attitude as in that of the Englishman. On many Irishmen the sight of a man crossing himself at the Angelus bell has the same effect as, on their neighbours, the sound of the word " Pardon " or " bye-bye." It is not true, as is often said, that all the gentry in Ireland are Protestants: most of the gentry and many of the half-gentry, would be nearer the mark: but there is a cachet to being a Protestant, to knowing Protestants, to having a Protestant on your Board of Directors, that is curious among people still half inclined to believe that all heretics must eventually frizzle in hell.

This social aspect of the religious cleavage can be studied with profit and amusement in the Big Houses, at least in those of them that have not yet been acquired by religious orders or by the State. The owners are staunchly Protestant, more by reason of class, sentiment and tradition than of deep religious conviction, the Reformation, the Bible, the Crown, their school and regiment, all hazily merging together in a conception of what's what for which they are prepared at any moment to shed their blood. It is the proper, in fact the only, thing for a gentleman to be, they imagine, just as it is taken for granted that the people employed about the estate will be papist, Popery being, to their minds, an affair of the kitchen and stable.

A more delicious comedy than when some recent English convert arrives in a house of this kind for a visit, it would be hard to imagine. I mean, of course, a convert of the usual type, employed in the Foreign Office perhaps, intellectual, musical, cultivated to his finger-tips, a good European and a ballet fiend. It is highly diverting to see dear Nigel or Derek troop off to the parish church with the cook and the maids and the gardener, and to hear the anguished protests on his return. *The sermon was quite extraordinary and O my dears, the smell!* The suavities of Father Rothschild, S.J., had made it all appear so very different. His host will go to church later in the morning too, because the Protestants must keep their end up and because the Rector, whom he may bring home to lunch, is a decent old boy. The church he goes to is older and handsomer than Nigel's but there are only a handful o people in it. The music is played on a reedy organ by the Rector's wife and in winter it is bitterly cold, no funds being available for the repair of the stove: he shivers through the service, joining dutifully in the growl of " Almighty and most merciful Father, we have erred and strayed from thy ways like lost sheep " and thinking the while that he must really do something about those fences before another of his rams falls into the sea: and, in the days before the Republic was finally and positively and legally declared, he would have sung " God Save the King " a little defiantly at the end.

His views on Catholicism are as sharp and precise as his attitude to Protestantism is emotional and vague. He is aware of a Popish plot to creep in everywhere and finally seize power, if it takes them a thousand years. " Take Britain: they've got the Foreign Office—look at poor old Nigel—and they'll be getting the Army next. I tell you, they stick at nothing." And if you were to draw him out, not a difficult matter, for once embarked on this subject he displays a fine nervous fluency greatly at variance with his normal habits of conversation, you would find he has fully considered the measure that ought to be taken.

Turn 'em out ! Turn 'em all out ! Of everywhere !

" And what would you say, Charlie, to putting 'em against a wall ? "

Mmm . . . shouldn't do that: don't say but it mightn't be for the best: anyway, turn 'em all out. Before it's too late.

But he would probably make an exception in favour of

the local parish priest, who knows a horse when he sees one and with whom he has often cracked a bottle: and who does, he must say, keep the people in excellent order.

The moral cleavage is wider and deeper than the social, even if in its origin it is social too. The Protestant morality, truth telling, word keeping, fair dealing, is the morality of free men everywhere: its honesty, its scruple in business matters, the morality of those who have never known the extremes of want: its loyalty and courage, the morality of those accustomed to lead. It is simple, sufficient and, without touching the heights of spiritual beauty, appealing. Catholic morality is more subtle and more complex, its subtlety and complexity being such, indeed, as often to cause one to wonder if it exists at all. The virtues listed above are of course smiled away as examples of Protestant naivety: what are hard to discern are those which the Catholics put forward in opposition. Forbearance, compassion, humility, the grace of lowly people, occur to the mind, but no sooner have they done so than one begins to reflect that the very opposites of these qualities are present equally. Some Catholics are pleased to see in their moral ambiguities the proof of one more superiority over the Protestant. He is crude, obvious, all of a piece, unlike their interesting and complicated selves. It may well be so, and yet it is arguable that they are even simpler than he, with the simplicity of a pool of bog water, reflecting now the radiance of the sky and the colours of the mountains, now the image of a cow wandering past its edge, and now again remaining perfectly blank, as the weather changes.

The Catholic in Ireland, then, distinguished himself from the Protestant not by virtue but rather by his lack of it: not by his behaviour, but by his point of view. And this is not surprising because the Church herself sets no great store by virtue. Organization is her business and very capably she attends to it. When first I came to know Ireland I was

dismayed by the conduct of many of the bishops and clergy
because I had a mistaken idea of what their function was.
Their arrogance, their pride, their vindictiveness, their greed,
did not square with what I took to be the mission of a
Christian priesthood. But after time had passed I began to
see the error. I perceived at length what Yeats and his friends
had meant when they declared all bishops to be atheists.
They did not believe themselves in what they said: their
sermons were entertainment rather than edification, and
duly taken as such by the faithful. They were not following
the Way and the Truth at all; they were running a country.

Beside me as I write is a copy of an Irish newspaper,
containing a pronouncement by a member of the Hierarchy,
which ends with the following plain words:

"I have said that the teaching authority of Bishops
includes the right to determine whether faith and morals
are involved, so that one cannot evade this authority
by the pretext that they have gone outside their proper
sphere. A familiar pretext in this connexion is that
the Church has no right of interference or guidance
in political or social activities. It is unfortunately
necessary for me to say that this is a grave error, and
that it is opposed to the explicit teaching and practical
action of many of the Popes. God is the author of
organized civil society as well as of the individuals who
compose it, and hence political and social activities,
quite as much as those which are purely personal and
private, are subject to God's moral law, of which the
Church is the divinely constituted interpreter and
guardian. It is the province, then, of the Church's
hierarchy to decide authoritatively whether political,
social and economic theories and activities are in
harmony with God's law; but it is outside of their
sphere to determine amongst approved theories and

systems which is best calculated to promote the temporal welfare of the community."

The reverend gentleman was addressing the senior boys of Rockwell College, and the particular point which gave rise to his general statement, and which he was concerned to drive home to them before they went on to their higher education, was that no Catholic might " under pain of grave sin " attend at Trinity College, Dublin. Trinity College is a Protestant seat of learning, and it is felt that attendance there must be detrimental to the faith and morals of Catholic youth. If the primal arguments are accepted, this may seem right and proper enough: but the curious fact is that quite a number of Catholics have studied at Trinity with the full consent of their spiritual overlords. To the riddle " When is a grave sin not a grave sin ? " the reply will suggest itself, " When it suits the Bishop to say so." In other words the Bishops do not believe all they say, which to some minds will seem right and proper too.

The same principle was invoked, and in a still more puzzling way, when the Hierarchy decided to suppress a welfare scheme put forward by a young and unusually active Minister for Health a year or two ago. The young man had already in three years of office done notable work in fighting tuberculosis and now had prepared a scheme that should offer to all Irish mothers free care during their pregnancy and confinement. He had the support of the Government, the Trades Unions and most of the fairminded and decent people of the country, while many of the doctors fought him tooth and nail. And suddenly, overnight as it were, the scheme was stopped and the young Minister was asked for his resignation. He was asked to resign by the Prime Minister, who had approved the scheme, at the suggestion of the leader of his own party (the Government then being a coalition) who had never opposed it. There, like so many strange things that happen in Ireland, the matter might have rested, sunk in the mists of rumour and speculation. But the Minister had rather more character than the run of Irish politicians. His colleagues exclaimed in bitterness that he was less of a gentleman but a long and devoted study of Dail personalities persuades me that here they were wrong. At all events, he gave the story to the Press; and the country learned with interest if not with surprise the exact procedure followed by their Lordships when faced with social legislation likely to strengthen the hand of the State at the expense of their own power.

They declared quite simply that the scheme was contrary to Catholic teaching. A scheme of the kind could never go through without the approval of God and only they, as once again the faithful were reminded, were qualified to say whether God had given it or not. As it happened, He had not, showing Himself on this occasion at least to be in full agreement with the medical gentlemen in Fitzwilliam Square. What God disliked most of all in it, the Bishops at first declared, was the provision made for the sexual education of people about to become parents: but the Minister took the wind out of their sails by announcing that he was ready to meet their wishes in this respect. After a further con-sultation with the Deity, the Bishops revealed that His main objection, after all, was the absence of a Means Test. And it is here that the mind reels and imagination boggles; for while we might conceivably accept the fate of poor Irish women, the yearly pregnancies, the loss of children through ignorance and poverty (*Welcome the Will of God!*), the too early old age, as all a part of the Divine Plan, by what leap of fancy may we include the Means Test in the same?

There is no need for us to do so as no pronouncement has yet been made *ex cathedra*. It may still come, felicitously timed perhaps to coincide with the excavation of a new and authentic version of the Gospels, revealing that no one in fact was healed until Our Lord was satisfied that he was without means of his own. Until that day we are free to make of it what we can, we rest on our bewilderment. But the bewilderment continues only while we persist in trying to find a religious motive for the Bishops' action. Once we accept the fact that they are ruling a country, concerned as all rulers are to prevent authority from passing to others, the picture clears and we all feel wonderfully better. For as rulers, as administrators, the Bishops are not too bad. Most people would rather endure their sway than that of a Communist Party. Do exactly as they tell you—it is sometimes reasonable; pay them what they ask—it is not always excessive; and you can live in Ireland happily and at peace.

But no matter how well-intentioned a despot is, he can in the nature of things tolerate neither opposition nor criticism. Rebels have to be put down, not always at once, but with sure and relentless efficiency. The cry of the Prime Minister " I will obey my Church even if I lose votes by it ! " at a ticklish moment of the Mother and Child scheme wrangle described above, was magnificent; but he forgot to add that if he disobeyed her he would be dished completely. Here again, a curious impression is created on the outsider. It is strange indeed in a land for ever vaunting itself as a Christian democracy to hear people lower their voices and see them look nervously over their shoulders when certain subjects are mentioned. It is not only strange but, on the face of it comic, for there seems to be none of the apparatus which in other countries makes such a mentality understandable. There are no uniformed thugs, no concentration camps, no imprisonment without trial. Yet sometimes in the uneasy, haunted atmosphere of Ireland one could fancy oneself away in Madrid; and one is strongly put in mind of that affecting poem, or ballad, of the little girl hastening through the twilight pursued by ghostly feet, afraid to look over her shoulder, her terror mounting with every step she takes until at last, safely home, she turns, and sees a donkey.

The night before I left Dublin for Cork I had been with a party of French people who were anything but amused. They were in a condition of mazed incredulity that was pitiful to see. They had come from Paris to make a film on the electrification of rural districts with special reference to the part played in it by American dollars. The work should have taken three weeks and in their precise French way they had made their plans accordingly: but one mishap followed another, some of the equipment was faulty and could not be repaired in Ireland, people did not turn up as arranged or the weather was unsuitable for shooting. The weeks slipped quietly by and here they still were, marooned on cloud cuckoo Island, with the soft patter of rain in their ears and plenty of time to consider the life around them.

" It cannot continue ! " said one of the ladies, with finality.

" Oh can't it, though ? I'm afraid you're mistaken," said a native.

The lady shook her head with indulgence. " Non ! ça ne peut pas continuer. There will be revolution."

" I wish I agreed."

" No, because it is logical that it will not continue. It is impossible, you see, in the modern world. There will be revolution before very long. Of that I am persuaded. Oh ! and by the way," she cried in sudden parenthesis, " please tell me a little about sex in Ireland. We are always putting our feet in it."

The Irishman explained that his people were terrified of sex, life, sin, the Devil and each other. The French listened attentively as they might have done to an account of the habits of a tribe on a south sea island.

" Terrified of sex, très bien ! on connait ça," said the first lady. " But they are made the same as other people, no ? What do they do ? the men, for example ? "

The Irishman replied jovially that down in the country at least they consoled themselves with the sheep.

" And they are beautiful, your sheep, they are *vraiment* beautiful ! " cried another lady, on a note of applause.

" Eh bien, pour les moeurs, c'est évidemment particulier," said the first lady, with the civilized little French shrug that recognizes the extent and variety of the world. " But for the other matter, no, it cannot continue. There will be revolution."

Reason was on her side but reason in Ireland doesn't apply. At present the signs are for an intensification of Church influence rather than its decay. For timid uncertain minds which for all their shrewdness and brightness are little apt for sustained reflexion the cool assurance of the Bishops possesses a good deal of charm. The native caution also plays a part. Who knows ? it may all be true, about the flames of hell and that. Religion too has become a vested interest and piety brings in a handsome dividend ; and people speak of their relations as being " in religion " as one might say " in the grocery trade."

And yet the germ of a solution seemed to lie in this sleepy little grey town in County Cork. And the mind strayed further and turned with a real hungry longing towards the six counties of the north, cruelly and unjustly retained—so the legend runs—by the Saxon invader. Before the mind's eye rose a vision of the 12th of July with the boot-faced Orangemen striding in their thousands to the Field, all cold sober, to denounce Popery and its works and to sing the praises of the great and good King Billy for hours on end without flagging. Always a sincere anti-partitionist, in that moment I became almost a fanatical one.

God grant I may see the day when the barriers go down for the last time and the two states are merged in one ! and when these two engaging lunacies finally get to grips.

XII

ON TO KERRY

KILLARNEY was full of Americans in merrily coloured ties and attractive shoes. They were jogging through the streets in jaunting-cars, which they believe to be the native method of travel, or buying postcards, blackthorns, shamrock brooches and teapots with Killarney written on them in the many little shops which offered these curiosities. Now and again a lone defenceless one would be pounced on and kidnapped by a jarvey and carried away to see or do something interesting and expensive. A stream of traffic was proceeding in the direction of the Lakes.

I have never " done " the beauty spots myself since the day that some one blew a bugle at a particular place and charged me half a crown for it. That is the sort of outrage that can rankle in a bosom until life's ending. The man was never by me encouraged, still less invited, to blow his bugle. The point of the action, it was explained, was that the bugle's voice would echo; but since I do not care for the sound of bugles at all, this was merely an aggravation.

No doubt the Americans have to pay seven-and-sixpence for the same little treat and no doubt they would think it cheap at the price. The dear souls put up with amazing extortions with the best and sunniest grace in the world. Sometimes they can be heard inquiring of each other why they don't buy a house in this lovely place and settle down right here among all these lovely people. Killarney appears to bind them in a spell.

A friend of mine was accosted by one of them, a large

lady bun-faced and bespectacled and tremulous with nice feeling and good will. In one smooth pink hand she carried a Madonna lily.

" Will you pardon me addressing you ? " she demanded. " Do you know where I can find a Catholic priest ? "

What with one thing and another he was inclined to fear for a moment that here was a case of religious mania; but the lady hastened to set his mind at rest.

" I'm not a Catholic myself although I have nothing in the world against it, Catholics very often are lovely people some of my very dearest friends are Catholics but what's happened a lovely Irishman just gave me this lily right out of his garden here in Killarney and I was so moved by his gift I said to myself Amelia ! just you go right on and find a Catholic priest and have that lily blessed."

My friend made suggestions for the carrying out of this clearly reasonable plan and she went on her way, the lily waving jauntily in her hand. Presently she returned in high feather and sang out to him from the other side of the road.

" He blessed that lily ! " she cried. " And do you know what ? I'm going right on back to the hotel and press it. It's been blessed and now it's gonna be pressed ! Blessed: pressed. See ? Oh I sure do love Killarney."

Leaving the Americans to their own devices and rewards I went off to the best hotel for luncheon. There they brought me a morsel of fried plaice with a dab of sauce alleged to be tartare, some strips of grey boiled mutton with carrots and potatoes and some chocolate " shape." And suddenly as I toyed with this culminating delicacy my mind was flooded with the sweet reminiscent nostalgia that Proust felt as he munched his little cake: only I, not having the analytical powers of that genius, could not immediately determine to what " things past " it referred. Presently however the light dawned on even me and I recalled that almost exactly a year ago on a beautiful summer day I had sat in this same room and eaten exactly this same meal crumb for crumb.

From the next room where a wedding breakfast was in progress came voices rising and falling in bursts of oratory, interrupted by delirious applause. Then a reedy wavering tenor launched solo into "Mother Machree" and this again was followed, with some little confusion of idea, by "A Nation once Again" and "The Boys of Wexford." I paid my six shillings and sixpence and moved to the bar, pursued by a tipsy press photographer who thought I was connected with the bride. The mistake being finally brought home, he sat cosily down at my side and began to relate in some detail the story of his life; and, having an hour to spare before my train left, I eagerly drank it in.

I was going to spend a few days with a friend of mine who lived in a delightful house beside the seashore at Kells Bay. A remarkable thing about this lady was that although most of her life had been spent in Scotland or England, she fitted with entire success into the Irish scene. She had moved from London after the war like so many others; but unlike so many, and indeed most, others she had never for a moment been at a loss.

The sufferings of some of the English immigrés into Ireland make pitiful hearing. Even on the material plane they were grievously deluded as to what was in store. They expected to find a comfortable old-fashioned country with plenty to eat and plenty of servants, and where gentlemen's residences with land attached could be had for a song. They were under the impression that the cost of living was low.

Plenty of food there certainly was: the trouble was to find some one with more than the vaguest idea of how to prepare it. The austere and puritanical Irish are as indifferent to good cooking as to all the arts of civilized life. Like all the truths concerning Ireland, however, this must never be put

down in black and white. A colleague of mine was rash
enough once to write a provocative article on the subject;
he drew the usual storm of abuse down on his head and one
reader was so incensed that she challenged the luckless
fellow to a meal in her house. The editor of the paper
insisted on his taking her up; and in an atmosphere fraught
with nervous tension he consumed a leaden omelette, soggy
chips and some yellowish tinned peas. The reader's husband,
in a disloyal aside, expressed satisfaction that the ordeal was
over as she had been practising her omelettes on him ever
since it was mooted; and the journalist, in a follow-up, duly
admitted his error.

People describing themselves as butlers and parlour maids
also came readily forward but seemed to bear no relation to
what their foreign employers understood by the term.
Humanly speaking, most Irish servants are admirable. They
are pleasant and willing and friendly: they do not take
umbrage or declare that something is " not their work ":
they rise splendidly to an occasion and triumphantly
surmount a disaster: they are charming conversationalists,
like most of their race, and often the sagest of counsellors.
But they do not understand a well-regulated household on
the English plan. The idea of meals being served always at
the same time appears to them as a foolish fad. They will
wipe the oil-lamps with the monogrammed damask and stir
the pig-food with the Georgian spoons if these chance to lie
handy. They are not in the least resentful when their
mistakes are explained, but gently repeat them at the first
opportunity. Their employers thus could choose between
throwing up the sponge at once and spending all their time
and energy in merely warding the jungle off.

The widest gulf between dream and reality lay in the
field of acquiring property. Two native attitudes, the
public and the private, co-equal and co-existent as usual,

were to be discerned. The first was that the matter was one demanding the greatest caution. There appeared to be a danger of Ireland once again being invaded by the Saxon, this time using the insidious weapon of the cheque book. Large properties were passing into Saxon control and the Irish way of life, whatever that might be, was threatened. The Government, perhaps with the idea of slowing the process up but more likely to cut itself a slice of the cake, clapped on a stamp duty of twenty-five per cent for all alien purchases.

The second and private attitude was that here was a chance that should on no account be missed. Fears for the Irish way of life paled into insignificance beside the hope of disposing of some rambling decaying mansion for a fat sum to an innocent foreigner. Within a week of the stamp duty's introduction, experts were assuring their clients that there were at least three fool-proof ways of avoiding it; and as each property changed hands there was a licking of contractors' chops and a rubbing of builders' palms as they drew up their estimates for putting it into something like order.

" We'll sting them well!" they breathed: and so they did.

The surprise and chagrin of the new-comers were often considerable but their worries on the material score were as nothing to the confusion, the malaise, they experienced when they came to grips with the native mentality. They could never, honest souls, see the point of saying " yes " when you mean " no." To their minds speech was a means of communication: to the Irish, apparently, it was a method of concealment. The English liked, they could often be heard explaining, to know where they were: where were they ? They could not understand why the simplest transaction must be carried out in an atmosphere of positively oriental intrigue, in a web of move and countermove, for ever beyond

the power of their minds to unravel. The Austrians have an
ironic saying, "Warum einfach wenn es auch kompliziert
geht?": in Ireland it appeared to be the national slogan.

Again, many of the immigrants, while they had forsaken
their native land, still clung to its sturdy traditions. When
things were obviously wrong, for example, they had a feeling
that somebody ought to put them right. The custom of
blaming the Almighty for what with a little human effort
and plain common sense might have been avoided found no
cordial response from them. All too often they themselves
plunged bravely on into matters that even the angels might
have handled gingerly. Their endeavours were greeted with
respectful applause and smiling encouragement; only, in
some mysterious way, it all came to nothing. Whatever they
tried to take hold of seemed to elude their grasp with the
agility of a bead of mercury and they never could fathom
the reason why. They simply did not know, nor would it
have been in their natures to understand, the indifference,
the resistance to change, the saturnine pleasure in destruct-
iveness, that lay beneath the bland and charming surfaces.

No one could have been more English in her convictions
and point of view than was my friend: and no one ever got
Ireland's number faster or enjoyed the nonsense more.
Coming from outside and thus having no responsibility for
the general state of affairs, she could freely give herself up to
the pleasure of contemplating it. The tangled maze of local
politics, the obscure vendettas, the inter-weaving machin-
ations that set most English brains a-spin to her were as an
open book. Hardly a stone was thrown in her valley but she
knew the reason why. I ascribe this happy circumstance
partly to her study of the Middle East, for there is nothing
like a knowledge of the orient to prepare one for Ireland;
but whatever the cause it was a rare and splendid thing.

She was there to meet me as the little train panted into

Glenbeigh station and drew up with a grunt of satisfaction. Together we drove along the winding road to Kells with the mountains rising each side, changing their colour from blue to violet and then again to brown in the soft Kerry light. From time to time rounding a corner we caught a glimpse of dazzling sea. The hedges were gay with crimson fuchsia and between the grey boulders on the hillside the furze bushes glowed in the sun like countless tiny bonfires. Small white-washed homesteads stood out here and there, far from each other and from the road, austere and lonely.

As motoring in Ireland goes, the ride was uneventful. Nearly every one we met was driving on the wrong side of the road with the usual joyous abandon. Once we swung round a bend to find a little donkey asleep in the middle of the way with an expression of utter repose and trust on his face. Round another bend again there was a man stretched on the ground beside his bicycle, off which he had clearly tumbled, and breathing in great stertorous groans while a dog nosed anxiously round about. There had been a fair at Cahirciveen, it appeared; and when there is a fair in this part of the country it is the custom to transact the business, or most of it, the day before and to devote the fair-day itself to social intercourse and celebration. We considered whether it might not be best to convey the unconscious reveller at least to the side of the road and out of the stream of traffic; but reflecting that people in his condition were all too apt to turn nasty and to bite the hand that supported them, we left him to take his chance.

There he should lie, a silent witness to the Irish longing for oblivion. Is it this longing which causes them to brighten so noticeably when a death is announced? They have a vivacity on the day of a burial which is not seen on other occasions, least of all on those when it would appear to be more appropriate. Their music is harsh and sad, their interminable jigs are precise and athletic movements of the feet with the arms held closely to the side, the torso rigid and the face set in a dull severe mask; even their wooing is subdued and business-like. But as soon as any one dies a kind of electric shock runs through the community. With a beautiful precision work comes to a standstill. People flock to the bereaved house with an eager, intent look about them and bottles of liquor under their arm. Young girls follow the coffin to the grave with rosebuds in their button-holes, as if to a wedding. Female relations roar and bellow like wounded animals until the priest bids them settle down, when they fall silent again with a charming grace and every appearance of deep satisfaction. I shall always remember how a mother, whose child lay dying in a room upstairs, remarked that she would have to get the parlour chairs re-covered in time for the funeral. Death is a consummation to be wished, it would seem, and while awaiting it the wise man seeks the *piccola morte* that lurks in the flagon.

The end of the journey was drawing near and my friend was kept busy returning the greetings of passers on the road. Little barefoot children exquisitely pretty, flower-like in the delicacy and freshness of their colouring, glanced up with their shy gentle smiles; and now and again a collie would fling himself out of a cottage door and upon the car in a flurry of rage and with a passion of self-importance, as if trying to prove that even dogs in Ireland were slightly dotty.

We turned into a drive that ran under arched trees and beside a stream whose high banks, carpeted thickly with moss, spread a mysterious green gloom shot through by splinters of sunlight. A flock of turkeys emitted an indignant rattle as we passed them by. Out of the corner of one eye I observed Paphnuce, the earnest and resolute pig, working methodically on the tunnel through which he proposed at a suitable moment to escape from captivity. Hens ran to and fro, guinea fowl shrieked from the branches of trees, the blue squinting eyes of Siamese cats met ours at every turn, a small woolly dog stood on the steps at the front of the house courteously wagging her tail, and the old pink-washed house itself glowed in the sun against the background of trees, looking out over the waters of the bay to the undulating mountains beyond.

My friend Norah and I went for a stroll round the place before the sun went down. In many of the Irish country houses you visit there seems to be a steady downhill trend. A fence that you clearly remember from the time before has fallen down and not been put up: a window has been broken and starkly boarded over: or the front door bell no longer rings and has been replaced by a dinner gong or a trumpet. Here there were always improvements and I marvelled afresh at the energy and determination that must have gone into them. Norah had a horrible, indeed a ghoulish, taste for the flesh of limpets and often as we scrambled about the rocks on the shore, she would halt and, grasping her stick in both hands, quivering with concentration, poise it for an instant in the air: then with unerring aim and deadly power she would dash it against the doomed mollusc, neatly dislodging him and popping him into her mouth. The sight of this never failed to make me uneasy, yet filled me with admiration: and it was impossible not to feel that the qualities she displayed in these swift, brilliant little operations served her in larger matters as well.

As we went she regaled me with gossip, the delicious intimate gossip of small places that has a colour and a poetry withheld from the larger events of the world. There had been births, marriages, deaths. Some one had gone over the water and was sending home good money. A girl we knew had thought she was going to lose her grandmother. The old lady had been taken suddenly ill at eighty-two, which the family described as " the dangerous age ": but she had the good sense to put herself on a diet of whiskey and soon rallied and now, the dangerous corner rounded, looked forward to another long span of life. The old man of ninety-odd was still alive too, for he had a twin in another part of Ireland and was determined to see him stretched before passing on himself. They were going to build a new church, and there was a tax of a pound a cow for it. There was the usual ins-and-outs of local politics which it would be most imprudent—in fact, suicidal—to commit to paper.

I inquired for a certain gentleman from a neighbouring town who once wrote me one of the longest letters I ever received, even in Ireland. In an article I had lightly alluded to the fact that when we met he was mending the road and he took this as a sneer at manual workers in general and himself in particular. Having affectionately described me as a bitch, he went on to blast my article sentence by sentence, as a tedious preacher will sometimes take every word in a text one after the other. This accomplished, there came a sudden change of note: he began to complain, as to a well-wisher, of the scandalous way his selfless work for the national movement had gone unrewarded while others, less deserving, got jobs and pensions. I am always suspicious when I hear of patriots going unrewarded, since one has only to look round to see what plums have gone to men with nothing more glorious to their names than the shooting of a Tommy on a dark night or the burning down of an ancient country house; and in fact the inquiries I made failed to show that he had done anything for the Cause at all worthy of mention. I quote this only as a further example of what caution is needed in the appraisal of Irish statement and the reading of Irish history: for when first I read his letter I had assumed that his grievance was real and sent him a reply full of butter and honey and balm.

Norah assured me that my correspondent was still in the best of health and frequently to be seen about his business.

The evening wore on into a night of magical loveliness. Kerry is a land of mist and rain so light that it is hardly more than a moisture floating in the air, a land of blurred shapes and sudden vivid rainbows. The atmosphere is one of gentle melancholy, the characteristic smell, of clothes that are never really dry. In the rare and brief spells of hot weather it turns into a fairyland with the glow and colour of Italy and a soft radiance that belongs to itself alone. The inhabitants are in a strange way incompatible with it. If you compliment an Italian on the beauty of his country he cries enthusiastically, " Ah bello ! bello, no ? " and if you do the same to a Kerryman he remarks sourly that it is well enough for those that do not live in it.

The moon had thrown a path of silver across the bay and the valley lay sleeping in its light. Nothing was to be heard but the sound of waves tumbling on the shore and the chatter of the stream as it fretted its way over the rocks in its bed. We retired early, quite worn out with the exchange of news and information and, for my part, with laughing. If Norah in the midst of all her activity could make time to write down the events and impressions of her day, a magnificently comic book would be born: a book to sweep the cobwebs and rancours and lunacies of the Emerald Isle away in gales of robust, Elizabethan laughter.

XIII

A JOURNEY TO THE BLASKET ISLANDS

THE journey to the Blasket Islands was not a very long one in space. Every clear day I saw them from the garden of the house, over the blue waters of the bay, lying out in the Atlantic at the western tip of the Dingle peninsula, dark shadows on the sea. And then all at once they would be invisible, curtained off by the mist. A motor launch would have reached them in half an hour: they were barely twenty miles away as the crow flies. But there was no motor launch and the flight of Irish crows is of academic interest only and without relation to human affairs. There was nothing for it but to rise rather earlier in the morning than I care about and to take, as a beginning, the little green train to Tralee. To cover those thirty-nine miles the little train, pausing thoughtfully at each tiny station, took two hours and twenty minutes; and there was something fine in the leisure of its pace, in its refusal to be hurried, to take itself or its passengers seriously.

At Tralee a wait of three hours for the Dingle bus offered fresh opportunities for meditation; and at Dingle it was disclosed that there was no bus at all to Dunquin, thirteen and a half miles away and the nearest point on the mainland to the Blaskets. There was a bus to Ventry, about half the way along, but it went only twice a week. The local taxis were busy with a wedding or a funeral—in the excitement of it all I have forgotten which. But in Ireland people take an interest in their fellow beings, and never more so than when these are in some kind of difficulty. Their aim then is not only to soothe but to encourage. Urging me not to give way

to a facile despair, they led me to the Ventry-Dunquin road
and explained that if I would only start walking along it, a
turf lorry, a private car or a pony trap was sure to come by
—and that before I was fairly out of sight—and take me
wherever it was that I wanted to go.

How that Irish kindness, that friendly concern, does
warm the heart and ease the mind ! How rare, how precious,
it is in the world of to-day ! The glow of it was not
extinguished—not really—when five hours later I limped
into Dunquin with the skin off my heels and a vague sense
of having absent-mindedly filled my suitcase with lead. In
all that time I had not seen a solitary vehicle, and hardly
more than a dozen men working in the fields or on the bog.
A young man let me rest my bag on his donkey's back for
the time that our ways ran together and entertained me with
stories of how the 'flu had carried off all the old-age
pensioners the winter before: to the satisfaction, he assumed,
of the government fellas in Dublin. And once I went into a
little pub by the wayside and asked for a glass of rum to
revive my spirits. The old lady behind the bar was
incredulous.

" Rum ! You never said rum ! "

" I did."

" 'Tis terrible strong ! "

" I hope so."

" Did you ever take it before ? "

" I did."

The old lady looked me up and down and called to
someone sweeping the yard outside, " Mary ! Come in,
will you ? She wants rum."

Mary came in and said, " And isn't she right ? Isn't
rum a very fine drink ? "

Warmed by this tolerance, I explained my difficulties
and she cried, " Now isn't that the divil ? You missed a

ride with the schoolmaster by inches. You'll never walk it, mind."

And many times in the long hot afternoon I thought I agreed with her. But trudging along on that apparently endless road I saw things which, inside a car, I should certainly have missed. At the end, the very end, it ran up a mountain and down again; and pausing on the saddle with the busy little mountain breeze cooling my ears, I looked back the way I had come, and there were the many rounded peaks of the Kerry Hills swimming in the blue haze of evening, wave upon wave of them, more beautiful than they had ever seemed before, remote and mysterious as the mountains of the moon; and I looked forward down the last lap to the cottages of Dunquin, with the Great Blasket Island lying three miles out like a fat, tawny seal in the fading sunlight, and beyond it, An Tearaght, shaped like a bell, rising from the water with the subtly enchanted air that hangs about the rocks of Leonardo da Vinci.

A whole day had passed in covering the eighty miles round the shores of the bay, and the slow painful method of it was perhaps a better one than shooting across the water in a boat. The world I was entering was separated from the one left behind by more than a twelve-hour journey. Gradually the little cottages dotted about on the hillsides had grown fewer, looked poorer; the faces of the people became harder, more finely modelled; the flowers, the blarney were forgotten, speech became direct and candid. It was an austere, a bitter world in which everything spoke of poverty. Even the animals looked weary of the struggle to get a living as they hobbled painfully along the roads, a front leg shackled to a back to prevent them from straying, and pulled hungrily at the meagre blades of wayside grass.

It was a dying world, too, inhabited by old people living on memories or young ones longing to be away. They could hardly wait, those young people, to exchange their simple, wholesome, laborious lives in that lovely corner of earth for the high wages and debased pleasures, the bustle and confusion, of an English or American town. To be sure, I was to meet that evening in Dunquin three bright young things who appeared to be thoroughly enjoying themselves: but they were not natives. One was a student from Dublin University; one was a vivacious young actress from the Abbey Theatre; and the third . . . dear me, the third! He came from the cottage where I was going to stay and greeted me, a young man in corduroy trousers and gaily checked shirt, with bristly blond hair and calm expressionless features. Surely I had seen that face, not once but many times, before? And yet I hardly expected to find it here. Gaelic streamed from the lips, uttered with the unmistakable intonations of the New World. Its owner had come from California, six thousand miles away, to learn the Irish language in one of the few recesses where it is still spoken every day. There was no particular reason for it, for he was not of Irish descent, and he could scarcely be hoping to further a business career in the States: his was the pure, disinterested passion of a real scholar. But I had to tell him I knew not a single word of it and, losing all interest in me, he retired at once, nor was the conversation resumed at any moment of my stay.

The undergraduate and the actress were learning Irish, too. He could not take his degree without it; it was as important to her career, and indeed rather more so than a talent for acting. There was something about the lively, business-like intrusion of people like these into a melancholy, shadowy, decaying outpost that was very comic; and something that was faintly macabre. Every year all through the summer they come and go, poking busily about in the relics of a dying culture. Reverently they copy into their notebooks the evening gossip of old fishermen, with awe they hang upon the prattle of tiny tots: and at the end of it all the little gold ring goes up on their lapels, they are Irish-speakers now and voilà! they have one more qualification to become an egg-tester or a pathologist, an inspector of taxes or a politician, at the earliest opportunity.

I had not come to study this, however, but to pay a visit to the Blaskets before it was too late. For in a very short time the Great Blasket Island, the only one of the group that is inhabited, will be empty. The people are moving to the mainland as fast as they can find houses there to receive them: it is not very fast, but there are barely thirty of them to come. You hear different reasons for their flight. Some say it is because the fish have moved away to other seas. Once upon a time a family could live on the fishing, if they also had grass for two cows. Others say the weather has changed and the winters are fiercer, so that the island is cut off for weeks at a time, whereas in their youth the mail and the provisions could always be rowed across at least once a week. And others again simply say that the minds of men have changed, and they will no longer bear the hardships that their fathers accepted as a matter of course.

There was a cloudless sky next morning and the sea was a brilliant cornflower blue. I perched on a rock and waited for the island postman's canoe to put out to sea, coming to fetch the letters and ferry me back with him. But he never came that day, nor the next, nor the one after that. In fact, he telephoned to the mainland to say he should not come at all until the wind had dropped. It began to look as if I must pass my summer lying on the rocks and peering out to sea, shrivelling in the sun like a stranded fish. It did not seem possible that the weather could ever be finer or the sea calmer. At last I was driven to make an arrangement with a local man, which I had hoped to avoid, for if there is one thing the simple Kerryman likes better than a little easy money, it is to make a fool of a stranger. He was a fine, upstanding young fellow with honest blue eyes that looked straight into mine, and the sum that he named was a small fortune. He pointed out that it was little enough and that only the summer before an American gentleman had cheerfully paid twice that amount. Saying that I would think it over, I retired to consult a woman of the islands now living on the shore and to whom I had been introduced by one of the clergy: two good reasons for expecting a valid opinion.

"God forgive him!" she said, clapping a hand over her mouth, and at once added the eternal Irish formula, "I haven't said anything, now, mind you."

So I told the young man I should wait for the ferryman after all; but after a protracted negotiation, oriental in its ruse, its use of the go-between and its careful preservation of face on both sides, a bargain was struck with neither party feeling too badly.

The prudence of the island postman became a little easier to understand when I saw the craft in which we were to make the voyage. She was long and narrow, made of nothing but tarred canvas stretched over a delicate wooden frame, and she danced about on the waves as light as a feather, or wriggled uneasily if any one made a move. We shot out over the clear green water, past the black jagged rocks with white surf foaming angrily at their base, and made for the open sea. The two boatmen laughed and sang and made jokes with each other as their oars flew through the air as if, after all, to leave their little farms or potato patches, their digging or turf-cutting for a few hours was not quite the grave matter, the harm to their interests, they had thought it might be when we discussed the fee: and in less than an hour they passed shrewdly between the two guardian rocks and pulled in to the runway.

It was not the right day to visit the island: you could not get a true picture of its life on a day like that. The people seemed to be the favoured inhabitants of a paradise. Sunlight twinkled on the water like a million gold coins set spinning; the little fields were bright with flowers; the air was full of the singing of larks and the lazy tumbling of the waves. The sea and the sky ran into each other in a blue that was deep and intense and yet radiant; the sand on the beach was dazzling white; and the whole scene, the islands and the rocks and the gently rounded hills far away over Dunquin had the gay, summery shimmer of Mediterranean lands. But no keen Latin minds were at work here to make the most of natural advantages. No luxury hotels or villas fronted the strand, no large ladies in striking beach clothes toyed with Cinzano beneath gaily striped umbrellas or gambolled with shrieks of merriment at the water's edge. Nothing was to be heard but the cry of birds and the sound of the sea, and nothing human seen but a few bent figures toiling on the land.

I went up the steep winding track into the village. The cottages were built on the side of the hill and with every turn of the track you found yourself looking down on the roofs of those you had just passed. Many of them were in ruins, now, tumble-down crofts of coarse gray stone shouldering each other, miniatures of the ruins lying about all over Ireland. The little house where Tomás O'Crohan wrote his famous book, *The Islandman*, has been stripped of its roof and lies crumbling away in the weather; that of Peggy Sayers, another island author, is standing yet, but Peg herself was on the mainland where, blind and crippled, she kept her bed. The school, where fifty children once learned their lessons, is closed except on Sundays when the old people, who can no longer make the crossing to Mass in Dunquin, go there to say prayers. There was only one child on the island now; they pointed him out to me as something of a curiosity, a bright-faced little man sitting in a canoe on dry land and pretending to row. And the storytellers and the singers and all who made the renown of the island have long since disappeared.

I climbed still higher, up to one end of the village where lived an old lady to whom I was bringing a letter. She was only just out of bed and still combing her few white hairs, for these people are not early risers unless there are cows to be milked, and she had had to sell her cow the Christmas before. She spoke very few words of English but succeeded in making me understand that I was to come again in an hour's time when she would have cleaned the house and made the tea. And off I went, wandering about and talking to all in sight, and came back to find the kitchen as neat as a new pin, with a kettle singing on the hook over the turf fire and a place laid at table with an egg-cup and spoon, and my heart sank, for Ireland is greatly addicted to eggs and this one would make my third that morning. The kitchen was in harmony with the austere spirit of the island, being for all its cleanliness equally devoid of comfort and ornament; the floor was of stone and the chairs of wood, and the white walls were bare except for a holy picture or two, a certificate of the family's dedication to the Sacred Heart and a photograph of the late Dr. Robin Flower, the Irish scholar. It is touching to see how the islanders treasure the memory of that English friend of theirs. They speak as if it were only yesterday that he last came to see them, and ask at once if you are going to see the place where he is buried. In fact he was never buried at all, his ashes having been scattered from one of the island heights as he willed them to be; but in the eyes of the people the ceremony must have had something a little pagan about it, and they perhaps use the circumlocution out of affection for him and their good manners.

The kettle boiled at last, but my prayers succeeded and the hens refused to lay. The old lady was ashamed of them, but there was no help for it, and when I had finished my second breakfast she walked up with me to the top of the hill and we saw, glowing in the sun, the other islands, empty and lifeless as this one was soon to be. And we came down again, and she showed me her little estate, and the sheds with fishing tackle and tools and freshly cut wands of pussy willow that her sons made into lobster pots, when they came back from their day on the bog, cutting turf. Then we had to say good-bye, good will being no substitute for language, and real communication between us being impossible.

On my way down to the tiny harbour a fine young man with dark curls and a broad white grin called out to me; and I confessed, yet again, that I had no Irish, and he replied at once that I was very much better without it. And he went on talking in the beautiful lively English of native speakers, saying how much he wanted to go away, and what a wonderful place must London be, and lamenting that there were no girls on the island. " No girls at all, think of it," he said, gravely: and I did think of it, and of him, too, of his charm wasted among the seagulls there and of the brilliant position in a Dublin government office which, with his mastery of the Gaelic, he might have been filling.

The boatmen rowed away over the sparkling sea. I had paid my visit to the Great Blasket Island, the first and perhaps the last. It may be that when I come this way again I shall hear that all the islanders have found the homes they are looking for, and have been absorbed in the life of the mainland. And mingled with the relief of greater comfort and greater security, there will be a melancholy, a sense of having fallen from high destinies: for the islanders share in the human passion for being a little special, a little different from the man next door, and the kindly disparagement in their voices as they speak of the mainland folk is delightful to hear.

I had not been with them when the weather was wild and the wind screaming round their lonely cabins; or when some one fell ill, or a woman began labour, and the doctor could not cross to them; or when the body of one of them was recovered from the sea. Unless one had, one could form no idea of what it is like to be a Blasket Islander. But I carried away a memory of friendly, courageous people, civilized with none of the aids of civilization, yet primitive enough to have kept the sense of wonder, of awe and reverent delight in the natural world alive in their hearts: accepting the end of their way of life with philosophy: indulgently amused at being the object of interest to so fortunate a being as an outsider.

XIV

IRISH PILGRIMAGE

I HAD returned to Dublin from the land of enchantment with the firm resolve of settling down and doing some useful work; but it was not to be. One morning at twenty past eleven there came a ring at the front door and it was a ring that held an unmistakable note of doom. Trouble rings at a doorbell in a manner peculiar to itself and in Dublin the ear becomes sensitive to it. I stood in the hall for a minute or two, eyes closed, in the attitude of prayer: then bravely opened.

A young man of my acquaintance named George stood on the steps outside. At the first glance there was nothing unusual in his appearance. He was dressed in an old frayed tweed jacket, with volumes of poetry thrust into the pockets and stains of red and yellow where the fried egg and tomato on which he lived had cascaded from his fork: baggy, wrinkled trousers of another kind of tweed: and shoes that apparently were never cleaned or unlaced. His matted hair rose stiffly above the poetic forehead like scrub on the brow of a hill. His fingers were orange with nicotine. But the wildness in his eye was not the wildness to which all who knew him were accustomed; it was a new, desperate wildness; and he was shivering all over, like a colt about to run a race.

" I've been evicted ! " he cried, and there was a note of heartbreak in his voice.

" Evicted ? "

" Evicted. There's been an eviction."

Then it was that I saw he had not come with empty hands. Dumped on the ground beside him were two fat fibre suitcases, tied with string; a wooden grocer's box filled with books: and a cricket bat: and my blood ran cold.

" You'll never leave me sleep on the street," he pleaded. " It's only for a day or two. There's money coming. . . . You've plenty of room up there," he explained.

It was true there were two spare bedrooms in the flat. It was the only real drawback the place had. I stood there, eyeing him doubtfully.

" Surely you won't close the door on an evicted man ? "

I opened it wider at that and the evicted man carried his possessions inside. He bade me hold on a second while he brought up the rest and, looking past him to the street, I saw a wheelbarrow laden with more books, crockery, shoes and a frying-pan waiting quietly on the other side of the hedge. This he pushed readily up the garden path, decapitating an antirrhinum here and there with a sudden little swerve as he took a hand off the bar to steady the contents.

" The barrow'll have to go back but there's no hurry," he said.

We moved the things upstairs to the flat. I tried grouping them all together in one place, in order to lend an air of impermanence to the arrangement, but he would have none of it. He unpacked everything most carefully and disposed the objects here and there and with his own hands carried the frying-pan, to which a piece of black pudding still adhered in a blob of grease, to the kitchen.

" Use anything you like," he said.

As soon as disorder was firmly established I took him into the sitting-room and opened a bottle. Very likely he had not breakfasted, for the whiskey warmed him and loosened his tongue in no time at all. He began to describe how indignities had been heaped on him in his lodgings for many a long week, culminating in a sudden demand that he should clear out at once; and when he asked for time, they had fetched a

Civic Guard. It was this brutal action on their part that led him to refer so constantly to the affair as an " eviction." The word cropped up again and again, uttered with a passion of bitterness that no mere skirmish with a lodging-house keeper could warrant. His expulsion had somehow linked itself in his mind with the sorrows of bygone days, the driving forth of the starving and dispossessed, the cattle-ship, exile. . . . You would have said he was suffering from a rush of ancestral memory, except that he came of an excellent Protestant family which had always ranged itself squarely on the side of law and order.

Presently it leaked out that he had paid no rent for a considerable length of time.

For some time past I had played with the idea of visiting Lough Derg. Strange and wonderful things were told of the pilgrims who flocked to the island there all through the summer. The religious life of Ireland is a fascinating object of study, taking up as it does a great deal of time and thought and newspaper space and having, apparently, no connection with behaviour at all; and at Lough Derg it could surely be seen at its most peculiar. The rigours undergone were severe to the point of barbarity: politicians, bookmakers, lawyers, publicans, droves of women were to be seen fasting, staying up all night, walking barefoot on sharp stones and proclaiming aloud their renunciation of the world, the flesh and the devil.

A kind of squeamishness had always held me back, caused me to delay the journey from year to year. The puritan which lurks in the heart of so many of us reveals himself in my case by a dislike of breast-thumping and religious display. I had no intention of renouncing the world and the flesh a moment before I must and therefore did not want to say I had, nor hear it said by others whom I believed—perhaps unjustly—to be in similar case. And mortification of any sort is repugnant to me.

The austerity of the programme, however, no longer appeared as forbidding when the alternative to it was sharing a flat with George. And as the day wore on and visitors for him began to arrive, this one indignantly demanding the return of the barrow, that one forcibly drawing attention to an outstanding account, I resolved to wait no longer.

A train leaves beautifully early in the morning for that distant and blessed spot in Donegal. It is full of pilgrims striving to fix their thoughts on heavenly things while the fragrance of bacon and coffee, prepared for others, is wafted up and down the corridor. I set out for the railway station in plenty of time and carrying the minimum of luggage. There wasn't a cloud in the sky: gently the sweetness of the summer day made fun of the gloomy enterprise ahead. An old countryman with black hair and flower-blue eyes and a face like a wrinkled apple approached and fell into conversation.

"I was never in Dublin before," he began, with the directness of a child. "Would you say the houses or the motor-cars were in the majority here? Ah, I could never drive one of them things. And if I could, the old woman (God rest her soul, she died two years ago: and me daughter's in the hospital this minute, which is why I'm here) would never get a moment's peace from the worry of it. So wouldn't you say things were best as they are?"

We lingered a little, discussing the point. The habit that many simple Irish people have of accosting a perfect stranger and laying some little matter before him is one that I have always found very charming; and I half hoped to miss the train. But, presently, having confided to me his belief that scientific discovery in no way made for human happiness, the country visitor moved on.

At the corner of Dame Street a car drew up alongside and blithe voices called my name.

" What on earth are you about ? Where are you going ? "

" I'm going to Lough Derg."

Loud laughter greeted the announcement.

" I am, you know."

"As an observer ? or a penitent ? or in a dual capacity ? "

" This is no laughing matter."

There was a fresh outbreak of ribaldry. I gazed at the occupants of the car in a placid, forgiving manner, as if already far above and beyond them.

" Well, jump in the motor, anyway. We'll drive you as far as Galway. After that, you can continue on foot with stave and script."

" This has got to be done in the proper way."

" Don't be silly."

The motor was a handsome and comfortable one. On the back seat reposed a luncheon basket, from whose gaping lid peeped forth the gilded necks of wine bottles and what, without wishing to examine them too closely, I took to be the legs of a cold roast fowl. Suppose that after all I went with the car as far as the west coast ? It would only mean one day lost and I could make my way up somehow to Lough Derg, through unfamiliar country. Perhaps, indeed, it was the wish of Heaven that I should accompany these friends of mine. Perhaps, impressed by the seriousness of my demeanour and the steadfastness of my intention, they would decide to join me on the pilgrimage. As we bowled away in the car I began to imagine the little scene: the embarrassed faces, the subdued tones, the " I say, would you think it an awful bore if we came too . . ."

" You'll be looking for a husband at Lough Derg, I suppose ? " sang the driver. " They say it's the place for it."

They had a long way to go yet.

The drive across the empty midlands began quietly

enough. From time to time one of us caught sight of a man working in a field and pointed him out to the others. Once we passed a lorry on fire, blazing away like a furnace while the driver and his mate sat on the bank in attitudes of contemplation. But when we stopped on the way for petrol the garage hand chanced to mention there was to be an amateur race meeting in the afternoon on a small course hardly fifty miles off our route or was it a hundred; and at once there was a feverish reorganization of plans.

The first race was only just run by the time we got there. The course was flat and very green with slopes covered with gorse rising up away from it and in the distance a line of blue rounded hills. Gypsies had moved up into position and now sat round their gaily coloured caravans in a little muddle of dogs, piebald ponies and children or patrolled the crowd soliciting alms with their own mixture of cajolery and menace. Fat cheerful ladies in shawls were selling oranges and slices of fat ham and cakes capped with horrifying pink ice; and a man strolled about with a basket of boiled pig's feet, followed by a swarm of attentive flies. In the shadowy interior of a voluminous tent a crowd milled about the bar struggling for glasses of stout as if their lives depended on it.

" Winner all right! Winner all right! " croaked the loud-speaker.

The cleavage of race and religion in Ireland shows itself in nothing more clearly than in the women's dress at such meetings. The ascendancy rigs itself up in tweed, sensible shoes and classic felt hats with Protestantism written all over them: the native element prefers feathered millinery, high heels and smart " costumes " of beige, mauve or emerald green. Both factions scorn to concede anything to the weather, so that on a wet day the daughters of Erin gradually take on the appearance of a flock of bedraggled hens and

on a warm one the faces of the ascendancy glow red as
boiled lobster. It was piping hot to-day; and under the
forthright hats the well-born faces, like scarlet lanterns,
added another delightful touch of colour to the joyous scene
before us.

We went to see the horses show their paces before the
second event.

"Hullo, you!" said a rich voice behind us.

It was the Brigadier: he never missed a meeting anywhere, however insignificant.

"Hullo, hullo!"

My two friends could not encounter anyone without
immediately attaching him in the web of their hospitality;
they began urging the Brigadier to drive over to luncheon
one day soon and proposed the following Tuesday.

"Can't manage Tuesday: it's Mallow," said the
Brigadier, gruffly.

Then how about the Tuesday after that?

"Clonmel," said the Brigadier, and now there was a
touch of real severity in his voice. It was plain that he was
unaccustomed to lightness in matters of such importance.

"I don't bet as a rule but I am going to have something
on that fellow there," he went on more kindly, as if trying to
put us at our ease. "Look at him! He'll do it on his head."
He strolled away humming, in search of the bookies.

The Brigadier is seldom or never mistaken where horses
are concerned. His choice was a bright, glossy chestnut
stepping daintily round the ring as if conscious of his worth,
while his jockey, a sullen youth, glared at the crowd from
under beetling brows. We decided to follow the matter up
and were discussing the amounts to be hazarded when
another voice broke in.

"I wouldn't fancy that one, reely," it said in a deliberately
casual sort of way.

The owner of this voice appeared to be addressing nobody in particular and had his eyes carefully fixed on a point in the distance.

" He looks a splendid animal."

" I amn't saying he's not. Only I wouldn't favour him," said the unknown, examining the horizon.

" D'you see the boy next him? He's from the same stable," he continued, and turned to go.

" And never raced before this afternoon," he concluded.

We looked at each other thoughtfully and as one man went to lay our money down.

" Take my tip? That's right," said the Brigadier affably, as we assembled to watch the race.

" Er . . . did you notice the young roan ? "

" Unknown quantity. Should do well."

They were off ! and a hush fell on the crowd. But hardly was the first corner rounded than it became apparent that something out of the ordinary was taking place. Three horses including the roan and the chestnut had drawn ahead and were easily leading the field when the chestnut's jockey began to pull. He pulled that horse as horse was never pulled before; he did everything in his power save wheel about and ride in the wrong direction. Yet it was all to no avail, for his mount was not content with the arrangement. The noble and sagacious beast knew that the race belonged to him and he meant to have it. His jockey was leaning backwards in the saddle and hauling as if engaged in a tug of war; but he calmly and steadily lengthened his lead.

The race was twice round the course, and one and a half laps were already completed. There seemed nothing for the jockey to do but bow to the decisions of his steed; but then suddenly he performed an act calling for a courage, an ingenuity and a selfless devotion that fringed on greatness.

Coolly he flung himself to the ground and swiftly rolled up into a ball with his white breeches pointing at the sky, while the others thundered past. The chestnut reached the winning-post riderless and humiliated: the race went to the roan.

Several moments went by before any one dared look at the Brigadier. His face had turned a good deep purple and his eyes seemed ready to spring from their sockets. The faculty of speech, never easy with him, was entirely gone; he stood rooted there, his mouth open, and stabbed the air with a denunciatory forefinger.

Presently he pulled himself together with an immense effort.

" Sorry about your money ! "

In a single rapid unspoken agreement we all of us forewent our winnings.

The afternoon had fallen apart and it was decided to push on to Galway with no further delay. The Brigadier asked for a lift in the motor, in any direction we chose, desiring only to be driven as fast as possible from the place in which things of this sort could happen. As we took our seats, and he clapped a flask to his lips, the loud-speaker gave utterance.

" Winner all right ! Winner all right ! "

" *Winner all right*," said the Brigadier and there were the disgusts of seven centuries in the way that he said it.

No sooner had the Brigadier left us, his lips moving in secret invectives, than my companions turned on me the full power and persuasion of their tongues. Why in the name of God, they wished to know, should any one go helling around barefoot and starving in company with some of the choicest rogues in Europe when they could just as well come and spend a day or two at a fishing pub in sweet Connemara, together with honest men ? The force of the argument struck me at once: Indeed, no rational counterblow suggested itself. We therefore proceeded on through Galway to Oughtarard where, having dined off cold salmon and roast duck and being flown with wine, we settled down with some kind new friends to a game of poker which lasted nearly all night. And the old tag about the shaping of rough-hewn ends kept flitting through my brain, and I gave thanks to the friendly Providence which supervised it.

One beautiful day followed another as in a dream. In Connemara one has a sense of being perched on the rim of the world. Dublin, that drowsy village, appears in retrospect as a roaring metropolis. It is a land of silences where nothing but the piping of larks, the mournful voices of seabirds and the splash of water is to be heard. The pointed purple-brown hills, the white cabins, the clouds passing languidly over the sky and the small black cattle are reflected sharply in the bog pools that lie still and bright as a sheet of glass. It is a land of silences, and colour. Here and there is a patch of brilliant green, a May tree or a chestnut: the rocks at the edge of the pools are festooned with shaggy golden weed: the piles of turf cut ready for the winter's burning are purple as the distant hills themselves.

It is also a land that is anything but friendly to human beings. A great deal of effort is needed to drag a living from its miserly bosom. There is little work for young men, none for girls, and away they go to England as soon as they can. The older people live as crofters, hoeing away at their potato patches and keeping a cow or two, acting as gillies to the fishermen and poaching a few salmon; and as they die off the locks are turned in the door and the small homesteads are left till they tumble down.

We met a vigorous and earthy old lady who sang us the threnody of dying Connemara. The evil, according to her, arose simply from the change in the people. They had grown too proud and lazy to collect edible seaweeds from the rocks as their parents did, or put out to sea to fish, or even to poach the rivers with the assiduity required if it were to be a rewarding enterprise. Soon the whole country would be empty as her hand. We asked if the Government had not some scheme for creating industry and she looked at us with the amused yet weary patience of country folk when their elected leaders are mentioned.

Despite the gloom of her forecasts, she was in the highest of spirits. She was toothless and the few remaining wisps of her hair stood up like the strands of a depleted mop. Her age, she believed, was about eighty.

" I'm a queer old hawk, am I not ? " she demanded.

Nothing would please her but we must come into the kitchen and taste her pancakes. It was a happy smoky Irish kitchen with a stone floor and wooden benches and chairs and a hook suspended over the open turf fire for the kettle or pot oven. There was a pub attached owned by her brother who, she informed us, God help him was as deaf as a post; and we asked her to give us some whiskey while we waited for the pancakes to be made. I give her method of serving it, for the benefit of English inn-keepers: it was to fill the measure to the brim and then half as much again, in case a few drops were spilled the first time and the customer did not get his proper share.

The pancakes were delicious, eaten hot with butter and sugar, one after the other in apparently endless succession. Mamo explained that English visitors would often come to her from the luxury hotels all round to get a bite of honest food. Some English ladies had come the year before that she hadn't cared for at all: they were fat old things with the shape gone from them and they wouldn't drink. No, she wasn't a fisherman: there was no tackle in the place and she'd have to whip off her petticoat and let it down in the water for a net.

" 'Tis illegal, anyway," she added, relegating this detail to its properly minor place.

We stayed on with her, helpless and incapable as satisfied boa constrictors, talking about the locality to her and her friends, who came in and out with charming informality. It was perhaps the quietness of life almost as much as the want of employment that drove the young away. A dance now and again, if the priest consented or some amateur theatricals, if the priest found time to take the rehearsals. . . . We asked her to tell us the local scandal but she said there was none, only what she created herself: and we'd never want to go into that. At last we took leave of the gay and spirited creature, promising to come again when we could.

I thought of Mamo and of her simplicity and gusto many times again that evening, as we fell in with two products of the New Ireland, a brother and sister. The boy was pale, spotty, with moist hands; he wore the badge of the Pioneers and sat drinking orangeade with an air of conscious rectitude. If any one addressed a remark to him his pinched face became scarlet and he performed while sitting a peculiar shuffling dance with his feet, at which he steadfastly gazed. The girl had won a scholarship from her local school to a convent, and then another to Galway University; and now, armed with a degree from this seat of learning, she was preparing to take London by storm.

She was dressed in a bright green suit and toeless high-heeled shoes studded with gold: round one ankle she wore a little chain and from the bangle at her wrist depended a mauve georgette hankie. She did not appear to share her brother's views in every respect, for she was drinking pink gin, daintily curling her little finger and casting her eyes upwards the while as if to mitigate the indelicacy of so natural an action.

" Pardon me ? " she would say, if anyone spoke to her.

Her favourite word was " essentially." She liked, she told us, essentially femi-nine clothes, essentially wholesome books to read and people that were essentially refined and intellectual. It was despair of finding these last in the wilds of Connemara that was driving her over the sea. On hearing that I was on the way to Lough Derg she said that it was an essentially moving experience, and her brother mumbled and blushed and danced a little in sympathy.

But was I really on the way to Lough Derg ? The time had come to face the matter squarely. It seemed to be now or never: I did not believe I should ever screw myself up to it again. Next morning at breakfast I announced my departure.

" Impossible."

" Why ? "

" Because we are all going down to Charlie's place for the week-end. You heard us telephoning about it. Don't be so silly: why must you be so silly ? "

Charlie lived about a hundred miles away to the south.

" What about Lough Derg ? "

" *Don't be so silly, I tell you.*"

They simply did not care if any one got to heaven or not—that is what it came to.

Soon we were heading across country for Charlie's place, thickly coated with white dust. After a short spell of fine weather the roads of Ireland become as dusty as those of central Europe at the end of a long and baking summer. It is one of her peculiarities, like the mountains growing wetter and boggier towards the peak, and the water coming out of the taps in a thin wavering trickle while the country around is more or less under water.

Charlie lived in a big Georgian house that was in urgent need of repair. Plaster fell from the outside walls to the ground in flakes and every now and again a tile slid easily off the roof. The stables, however, were always warm and dry and fitted with every convenience. Inside, the furnishings consisted chiefly of guns, spears, fishing-rods, swords and medals in glass cases, tattered flags and regimental colours and the stuffed heads and feet of large wild animals. There was also a table or so to be seen here and there in a clearing and a few chairs, hastily covered with chintz: and in the hall a huge chandelier, suspended by a frail wire rope from a hook, was grimly biding its time. Unopened letters were heaped on an old oak chest with rusty fastenings. As we came in a number of wolf-hounds rose and advanced, baring their teeth.

" Don't worry about them," called Charlie, as he came downstairs. " They're perfectly all right as long as you show no fear. Damn silly woman started flapping the other week: so they pinned her. Husband made no end of fuss, the old fool: need never have happened."

A curious aboriginal figure shambled forward out of some nook and, collecting our suitcases, made off with them.

" Mind if we have our drinks in the hall," said Charlie. " My bitch is just going to pup and I've made a bed up for her in the library. And we don't use the other rooms now, too much gear."

We all sat down in a corner of the hall while Charlie distributed tumblers of whiskey with a drop or two of water in it, and the wolf-hounds lay down to rest in a circle round us.

Charlie was splendidly all of a piece, as was clear from his conversation. The Government were all fools and knaves. He was not, however, referring to the Irish Government but the British. As far as Ireland went, he was apparently unaware of the existence of any government at all and could not for the life of him have listed the political parties: and should the name of some leading political figure crop up he would remark at once that he supposed the fellow was a " damned Sinn-er " and change the subject. His favourite story, and the only one of his repertory that was unconnected with sport, was of how some man had once tried to kick Mr. Aneurin Bevan's bottom on the steps of a London Club. He beamed like a cherub while the tale was unfolding itself. Only, just at the end, the light in his eyes would suddenly be extinguished, his brow would crumple and he would wind up sombrely: " Can't think how he came to miss him."

This was the second time I had been privileged to visit with Charlie. On the previous occasion he had asked me where my " place " was, and on learning that I had none, and that I neither rode, fished nor shot, he had lapsed into a bewildered silence. There was nothing in the least unkind or supercilious in his attitude; he was merely faced with something that was new in his experience. On learning more exactly what I was he had shown a civilized toleration, and had ordered a copy of *Moby Dick* to be placed beside my bed.

Throughout the week-end he spared no pains to make every one feel happy and at home Although much of his time had to be spent sitting with the bitch in the library, he did his best to see that we were entertained. We were taken to see the hounds and invited to watch as, yelping, they devoured some grisly carcasses. We were even allowed to drive with him and fetch some more carcasses, assisting him as he loaded them on to the brake. He walked us six Irish miles in the sun so that we could see with our own eyes the hedge that a fox, last autumn, had cleared in a single leap. He showed us a copy of a sharp note he had addressed some years ago to a neighbour, whose dog had worried one of his mares.

The rhythm of the day was broken by a series of

gargantuan meals which, except for breakfast, appeared at any time that suited the cook's caprice. Breakfast was always at nine because Charlie went in dread of his groom, who arrived on the stroke of half-past and would stand loudly muttering if he were a moment late. His meal invariably consisted of four boiled eggs, followed by four slices of ham and rounded with a leg of chicken or a chop or some little kickshaw, such as a pair of kidneys on toast. No one was welcome to speak until breakfast was finished: then with a hasty " must be off ! " Charlie leaped up and made for the hall-door with the wolf-hounds gambolling round him: and the rest of the party relaxed.

If there was one thing Charlie could never abide, it was the fidgets. He could hardly believe his ears when we told him on Monday that we should have to be getting along. We had arranged for the week-end, it was true, but he had taken that as meaning a fortnight at least. He pointed out that as yet we had done nothing: there were heaps more hounds and horses and notable landmarks to see and in a very few days the bitch would be ready to show us her family.

" Why, shooting will start directly ! " he cried. " You can't go before that, you know."

My friends explained that they were expected home, and that I was on my way to Lough Derg.

" Lough *Derg* ? " said Charlie. " Nothing doing up there, is there ? Much better stay for the shooting."

It is another peculiarity of Ireland that his kind of lunatic stands out there as wonderfully sane.

For my part I was determined to break away not only from Charlie but from my two companions who, I belatedly saw, were standing between myself and my true good. They had drawn me into a round of what I now perceived to be empty frivolity. I would leave them and go to Lough Derg across country, walking and begging for lifts and riding in buses, which is the nicest way to travel in Ireland and the best way of meeting her nicest people, who are the very simple and very ordinary ones.

Everything went as smoothly as if it were pre-arranged. A lorry carrying barrels of beer pulled up at my signal and the driver gallantly declared himself ready to drive twenty miles out of his course to further my ends. He was a smiling, rosy, comfortable person, but there was something he could not bear and that was England. He let a roar out of him at the sound of her name that would have wakened the dead. She had left a trail of death and blood and ruin in every country she ever went near: that was history. So distressed did he become, so wildly did the lorry career from one side of the road to the other, that I changed the subject and asked if he had any family, and he calmed down at once and smiled again and said he had two grown boys, thank God: they had beautiful jobs in Manchester and he was shortly going to spend his holidays there.

The next stage was by bus, at whose terminus the lorry driver dropped me with an invitation to look him up if ever I was in Kilkenny. The bus was a magnificent new one with shining rails and plump cushiony seats; but two minutes before she was due to leave the conductor asked all inside to change to a lesser and an ignoble one. The reason he gave was that we should be passing a town where a cattle fair was in progress and it would not be right, it would be asking too much, for the new bus in all the glory of her spotless paint to be dragged through the mud: a point which was readily taken and conceded by the passengers. Anxious to meet them, in his turn, the conductor arranged pauses in every town we went through for those who needed refreshment, and kept up a lively conversation on the way.

"You often travelled my route before! Don't tell me you didn't! Didn't I see you?" he said jovially to me.

"No, never. This is the first time."

"Then it must have been Maureen O'Hara!"

He was popular with every one in no time at all.

The best stroke of luck of all that day came as I was at luncheon. The waitress who brought my roast mutton and bashed turnip said she understood I was making my way to Donegal. Long ago I gave up trying to fathom the workings of the countryside grapevine, and now simply enjoy it and profit by it instead. There was a Protestant clergyman who was driving up all the way, the waitress revealed: he should leave at two and would be glad to give the lady a seat in his car. When ready to start, he was going to sound his horn.

This thoughtful piece of kindness turned out to be unnecessary for at about five minutes to two the noise of a violent collision brought us all running out on the street. The Rector, backing his car, had failed to notice the presence of a thick stone wall. Undismayed, he let in the clutch and brought his vehicle up to the front door in a series of frog-like leaps, peering benevolently through the window meanwhile in search of his passenger.

"Step in, step in, my dear lady: very pleased, I'm sure," he cried, cheerily. "We are going to have a lovely run, I do believe."

I settled myself beside him and we sped away to the north.

It was one of the memorable rides of my life, as much on account of the Rector's style of motoring as of his wholly entrancing conversation. The latter, what was more, had a powerful effect on the former: for example, when a point seemed to require emphasis he would remove both hands from the wheel and smash his clenched right fist into his left palm, the better to drive it home. He spoke of his parish, which had dwindled from five hundred souls to about twenty during his lifetime, and of certain forces that harboured designs on the rump of it. Only a short time ago they had claimed the conversion, on his deathbed, of one of his flock who lay in the last stages of delirium tremens.

" Death-bed conversion, indeed ! The poor fellow was out of his mind ! " snorted the Rector, sitting bolt upright and snatching both hands from the wheel.

" Aha ! but we diddled them over the funeral ! " he chuckled, gliding across the path of an oncoming turf-lorry. " We got up very early in the morning while they were still sleeping off the effects of their . . . their wake, and laid him reverently and properly to rest in our cemetery."

Somehow or other we got on to theology.

" Have you read Salmon on Papal Infallibility ? They've never replied to it: they can't," he cried gleefully.

Here he turned round completely, while I put a steadying hand on the wheel, and commenced to rummage about on the back seat for Salmon on Papal Infallibility.

" There we are ! " he said at length, giving the volume an approving little pat. " I make a point of keeping a copy handy. Take it, do. My address is inside."

For some little time after this he applied himself to the matter of driving. He waved gaily to all who passed on the road. He gave extravagant signals or none. He tacked to port and starboard as the fancy seized him. Nothing escaped his notice.

" Look at that, if you please," he said, as we sailed narrowly by a monument to some martyrs of the national rising. " Glorying in their shame . . . glorying in their shame . . ."

How sweet that old gentleman was, how simple and unaffected, how firm in his loyalties ! and, above all, what a fund of disappointed affection—one sensed—lay behind all his strictures.

" You must never speak the truth, my dear lady," he observed presently. " And you must never do anything on principle. That is, if you wish to be happy in Ireland."

I was fully aware of it.

Sooner or later, I knew, the moment must come when the Rector would ask why I was going to Donegal; and in due course he did, in the most delicate way, seek for information on this point. I hoped, I felt sure, that it would not mean the end of the sympathy that had so swiftly and delightfully grown up between us: it would be a little hard since I was in perfect agreement with all he had said. But on hearing what was to be my goal his jaw dropped in something like consternation and he immediately began to slow down the car. It looked as if I were going to be bidden get out and walk.

" I am afraid," smiled the Rector, after a short silence, " that you are not a very practical lady. You see, Lough Derg closed for the year last week. If you will forgive a heretic for drawing your attention to the fact."

And thus came to an end together all hopes of edification and all chances of seeing this peculiar and characteristic assembly for myself. A vision of that lonely, unpolluted lake rose before the inward eye, and I felt that affairs had taken a happy turn. Any opportunity for getting to know Ireland better should always and unhesitatingly be missed. It was with a sense of reprieve that I begged the Rector to allow me to accompany him, the wreck of my programme notwithstanding, and the dear fellow consented at once, with a complacent sidelong glance at Salmon reposing on my knee, like one who has just placed a time-bomb in an enemy stronghold. We shot dangerously forward once more into the golden afternoon: in no more appropriate way could an Irish pilgrimage be ended.